# RECIPES

*from*

## SWEET YESTERDAY

by
Thelma Allen

To Vicki —
you'll love Monica
for wanting you
to have all my
books.

Thelma

**RECIPES FROM SWEET YESTERDAY – Volume Three**
Thelma Allen

Second printing, March 1999
Third printing, November 2000
Fourth printing, October 2002


Published by:
**Sweet Yesterday**
**P. O. Box 111510**
**Nashville, TN 37222**

Author: Thelma Allen
Editors: Thelma Allen and Michael Allen
Graphic design/layout: Michael Allen
Illustrations: Sylvia Worcester
Cover photography: Michael Allen
Cover photograph models: Thelma Allen
        and her grandson, Allen Worcester
Kitchen in cover photograph furnished by
        Sylvia Worcester
Electronic Prepress: McPherson and Kelley, Inc.
Printing: Harris Press, Inc.

ISBN 0966832221

# TABLE OF CONTENTS

DEDICATION............................................iv

INTRODUCTION...................................vi

PORK.........................................................1

POULTRY................................................11

BEEF.......................................................25

FISH.........................................................41

FRUITS AND VEGETABLES.................51

DESSERTS..............................................67

COOKIES AND CANDIES...................139

BREADS................................................171

SALADS AND SOUPS.........................191

RELISHES AND PRESERVES...............205

MEMORIES...........................................221

# DEDICATION

I dedicate this book to my late husband, Marvin Allen. He was born in Jackson County, Oklahoma, in 1909 and passed away in June of 1996. We married in 1933 and operated a cottage beauty shop. By working together, we maintained a home with more satisfaction than most people have with both parents working. If there were little problems, and there were, we wouldn't have words before our clients. By the time we were alone, most of them weren't important anyway. We both tried not to have our misunderstanding in front of the children. I'm grateful to him for many things. We trusted each other. Many times we couldn't get off work at the same time, so he took the children to lots of ball games, rodeos, band concerts, youth camps, and just about every place they needed to go. If they had friends that need-ed a way home, they knew Mr. Allen would take them. In those days, kids called everybody Mr. or Mrs. Many times the car would be dangerously full of kids, stacked on top of each other.

Marvin, in our last few years of work, took lots of "little old ladies" home and was loved by all of them. Uncle Marvin was also a favorite of all of his nieces and nephews and his only sister, Zora. He was next to her in age. The oldest three in the Allen family were boys, then the girl was in the middle, and then the twins. The twins, Floyd and Lloyd, are the only ones living now; they are 86 years old.

Marvin never wanted to compromise, but sometimes we had to when it came to our needs, especially when it came to the children's education.

Marvin never crossed me on anything I wanted to do or wanted the children to do. If I mentioned anything I wanted or needed he got it for me, especially in the kitchen or little personal things. There were a lot of luxuries he couldn't give me, but he did give me love and support and no problems. I can be very thankful for that.

We had several nice vacations together while the children were at home. The children and I suggested the vacation spot, and that's where we went – no disagreement there. If we wanted to detour to see something, then we did just that.

Marvin did lots of cooking, did many dishes, ate many sandwiches, ran the sweeper, did the laundry, made the beds, and many other household chores, so I could devote more time on writing my first two cookbooks. He knew I was having fun, and it was time consuming, but not once did he complain. One of my biggest regrets is that Marvin didn't get to live and enjoy the last biggest boost in cookbook sales. He passed away on our 63th wedding anniversary.

**Marvin Ray Allen**

# INTRODUCTION

My purpose for writing this book is still the same as it was for my other two cookbooks. The older I get in this fast changing world, and the older our country becomes, the greater the need becomes for me to record these events for my children and posterity. These recipes and our way of life will be lost forever if not recorded. Life seems to get more complicated each day. I like to think, in most instances, for the better. I've seen lots of changes. I've gone through two World Wars, The Great Depression that lasted, you might say, 10 years. World War II took us out of the Depression with so many people employed. There were ships, airplanes, tanks, and artillery to build, just to mention a few. The people too old to go "off to war," grandpa, grandma, middle aged males and females did their part. We put our heart and soul in the effort to win the war, and we did! We had apple pie to fight for. We can't say "thank you" enough to those young men and women, both living and dead, who gave so much so we can have that apple pie.

There have been so many social and economical changes. We've gone from the horse drawn wheels to the motorized wheels on the ground, the small propeller airplanes to the huge jet-powered planes, rub boards to automatic washing machines, and clotheslines to clothes dryers. The list could go on and on, not to mention the men on the moon. I've seen bread go from 5¢ a loaf (six loaves for 25¢ on sale) to over $1$^{00}$ a loaf. I've seen cars go from $500 to $100,000. A used car could be bought for less than $200 that could be repaired by the owner. It was said that the Ford Model T automobile could be fixed with a tin can and bailing wire.

In my books I've described what farm life was like in those days, how we lived off the land and made do with what we had. We raised our own grain to make our flour, the corn to make our meal, food from the family garden, and the hogs and chickens for our meat.

My cookbooks portray self reliance, interdependence and a human spirit that will never be equaled, and it will make good reading for you and something for you to think and talk about. I have tried to simplify my books so the youngest and the inexperienced desiring to learn the art of cooking will get a driving urge to become the very best in that art. You will like my book!

I want to thank my children, Mike Allen and Sylvia Worcester and her family, my sister, Marie Mills, my old friends, and my newly acquired friends all over the world, and to those who gave me those wonderful recipes with their names and those without names. I also want to give thanks to the Lord who has given me guidance, strength and a long life enabling me to pass this pioneer history and recipes on to you.

# The Allen Children

Michael Allen

Sylvia Allen Worcester

Photographs by Marvin Allen

# PORK

# Aunt Lela's Fried Ham
## and Red-Eye Gravy

Aunt Lela was the eldest of eight children, the youngest being five months, when their mother died from pneumonia. She never married. She did all the things the pioneer women did, like making lye soap, watermelon rind preserves and molasses cookies, but she did it better. She could go into the kitchen and literally cook a terrific meal "out of nothing." Aunt Lela, no doubt, was the best cook ever.

After nearly all the children were gone, she began to room and board the school teachers. In the small schools, at this time, there would usually be three teachers. The principal, usually a male, would be married, and the other two, or maybe just one, would room and board at Aunt Lela's. The going price was $3$^{00}$ for board and an extra dollar for the room, and that was for a month. That wouldn't buy 1 meal now. It was a treat to go to Aunt Lela's.

Here's how she did the ham. She always sliced the ham real thick and fried it in a heavy iron skillet. To make the gravy, she left the scrapings in the bottom of the skillet. Leave the skillet on the fire, scrape the particles from the skillet and stir in the amount of hot coffee desired. Little red eyes will bubble up when the hot coffee is added, thus the name red-eye gravy. It was always served with those big fluffy buttermilk biscuits.

# BAKED HAM

Unwrap ham and place in a roaster fat side up on rack. Use no water and don't cover. Cook at 325° oven, allowing 16-20 minutes per pound. Thirty minutes before roasting time is up, remove from oven. Let cool slightly and cut off skin. It will be brittle and will come off easily. Score fat, stuff with whole cloves and brush with prepared mustard. Rub in about a cup of brown sugar. Pour off most of fat from roaster (use for gravy later) and return ham to oven. Bake for 30 minutes. Some like to add about ½ cup of pickled peach juice around the ham. Do not pour over ham.

# BAKED HAM WITH RAISIN SAUCE

8-10 lbs. ham
⅛ cup honey or corn syrup
¾ cup brown sugar
2 Tbsp. prepared mustard
⅛ cup orange juice
¼ tsp. cloves (ground)

Combine honey, brown sugar, orange juice, mustard and cloves over ham. Bake in covered dish for 1 hour. Then remove lid and bake another ½ hour. You might want to have your butcher slice it 1" thick to make it easy to serve. Serve with raisin sauce.

Raisin sauce:

2 cups water
2 Tbsp. brown sugar
2 tsp. sugar
2 Tbsp. butter
⅛ tsp. onion salt
1 cup raisins

Simmer 1 cup water, 2 Tbsp. brown sugar, and 1 cup raisins. Stir in 2 Tbsp. butter, ⅛ tsp. onion salt, the second 2 tsp. of granulated sugar for 10 minutes.

1 Tbsp. cornstarch
1 Tbsp. dry mustard
½ cup water

1 tsp. Worcestershire
¼ cup drippings from ham

Mix cornstarch, dry mustard with ½ cup water. Boil 30 seconds. Add Worcestershire sauce and ham drippings to raisin mixture. Serve with ham slice. You might add maraschino cherries for color.

## BAKED HAM WITH KRAUT

1 can sauerkraut (Bavarian)
1 ham steak (1" thick)
¼ tsp. celery seed
2 medium sized apples
⅓ cup molasses
1 tsp. dry mustard

Drain the kraut and finish the can with water. Mix the kraut and water, celery seed and arrange in the bottom of a greased shallow baking dish. Peel, core and slice the apples thin. Arrange the apples evenly over kraut. Lay on the ham steak. Stir the molasses into the dry mustard in a cup over the ham. Bake about 1 hour in a 350° oven until apples are tender. Cut ham into individual pieces and serve with kraut and apples.

# FRIED PORKCHOPS

2 lbs. of center cut porkchops
1½ tsp. salt
½-1 cup flour
1 tsp. pepper
½ cup milk
egg
cornmeal

Heat hot oil in a heavy skillet. Mix egg and milk together. Combine flour, salt and pepper. Dip porkchops into meal mixture; then coat with flour. Put meat in hot grease and cook 3 or 4 minutes, then turn and cook the same amount of time on the other side. To keep the coating good, then lower heat and cook until done. Not to make gravy would be a crime.

## BAKED PORKCHOPS
## WITH CARROT STUFFING

4 loin porkchops (1" thick)
1½ cups soft ½" bread cubes
¼ cup onion (chopped)
½ tsp. salt
¼ cup hot Dr. Pepper (soda)
½ cup carrots (grated)
1 egg (beaten)
1 chicken or vegetable
     bouillon cube

Brown chops until golden brown; reserve 2 Tbsp. of fat for stuffing. Place chops in shallow baking dish; sprinkle lightly with salt and pour ¼ cup Dr. Pepper around chops. To prepare stuffing, combine bread cubes, carrots, onion, fat, egg, salt, and the bouillon cube dissolved in hot Dr. Pepper; toss together lightly. Top each chop with about ⅓ cup stuffing and cover pan with foil. Bake at 350° for 45 minutes. Remove foil and bake for about 30 minutes longer. Serves 4.

No matter what the price is for pork roast, it's still a good buy. We can take advantage of sales and freeze it. Pork will freeze for 3-4 months.

## PORK ROAST

Boston butt is a good cut, 5-6 lbs. For the large family of that era, the larger roasts were cooked. Boil in water for about 1 hour. Remove from water and when cool enough to handle, slice in serving pieces. By doing this way, you can eliminate some of the fat. Save this broth to make corn bread stuffing or dumplings (use recipe from page 16 on dumplings). Place pork in large baking dish in layers. This makes it different. Sprinkle each piece with salt and pepper and a small amount of cornmeal. Bake at 350° about 1 hour.

# BARBEQUED SPARE RIBS

2 lbs. pork ribs
½ cup vinegar
2 Tbsp. brown sugar
½ cup catsup
1 tsp. dry mustard
⅛ tsp. salt
¼ cup lemon juice
2 Tbsp. Worcestershire sauce
1 tsp. paprika
1 onion (chopped)

Simmer all ingredients, except ribs, pour over 2 lbs. of ribs and bake for 15 minutes at 450°. Reduce to 350° and bake for 1½ hours. When eating these ribs, you'll think you have died and gone to Heaven. It's that good!

# HAM WITH ORANGE JUICE AND CATSUP

1 center cut of ham (divide
         into 4 servings)
½ cup orange juice
½ cup catsup

Fry ham with a little amount of bacon drippings, just enough to heat good. Don't overcook. Drain, add the combined orange juice and catsup. Place in oven, covered and bake about 30-45 minutes at 350° Don't let sauce boil away. Add more catsup or orange juice, if necessary.

# SAUSAGE BREAD

Heather Selby Nunez
DeSoto, Texas

1 can Pillsbury crescent rolls
1 lb. bulk sausage
1 egg
½ cup swiss cheese
        (shredded)
1 Tbsp. parmesan cheese
1 tsp. basil
1 Tbsp. parsley
1 egg yolk (for top to brush on)

Cook and drain sausage. Open dough flat and seal all perforation. Well floured board. Use rolling pin. Make 15" square. Add sausage to the top of the dough. Beat 1 egg with fork and add cheese, add to top of sausage. Sprinkle the spices and roll (jelly roll style). Place seam side down on cookie sheet. Brush top with egg yolk. Bake at 350° for 30 minutes. Can microwave after baking 3 minutes. Use fork to spread the cheese well.

"He that handleth a matter wisely shall find good; and whose trusteth in the Lord, happy is he."
Proverbs 16:20

# PORK LOIN POT ROAST

4 lbs. pork roast
2 Tbsp. bacon drippings
1 cup water
2 tsp. salt
½ tsp. pepper
½-1 cup flour

Trim all fat you can from roast. Fry in large heavy skillet or Dutch oven. Remove fat from pan and add the bacon drippings. Roll roast in flour and mix with salt and pepper. Force as much flour into meat as possible. Brown roast on all sides in the skillet. Add water, cover skillet and place in oven. Cook about 2 hours at 300°. To prevent roast from drying out, check at 30 minute intervals; add a little water if necessary. The last 30 minutes, add whole peeled potatoes and whole carrots.

# POULTRY

# Turkey

Turkey for Thanksgiving Day is as American as the Fourth of July. The Pilgrims served wild turkey on the First Thanksgiving in 1621, because it was in abundance. We use to eat turkey only on Thanksgiving, then we added Christmas and Easter. It's wonderful for picnics. You can roast it one day, cool and refrigerate, and take it chilled to the picnic the next day. Carve and serve at the picnic spot and let everybody make his own sandwich. Of course, it must be served with potato salad (see recipe on page 193). In most instances you can substitute chicken for turkey.

## How To Roast The Perfect Turkey

If the turkey is frozen, thaw unwrapped in the refrigerator 2-4 days. If shrink-wrapped, place under running cold water 2-6 hours, or until fowl is pliable. Rinse thoroughly inside and out with cold water. If you stuff the turkey, don't pack it. I prefer to cook the stuffing in a separate pan.

### Time Chart For Cooking Turkey In Foil

| Ready to cook weight (lbs.) | Appropriate cooking times (hours) | Internal temperature |
|---|---|---|
| 10-13 | 2½ | 165° |
| 14-17 | 3½-4 | 165° |
| 18-21 | 4½-5 | 165° |
| 22-24 | 5½-6 | 165° |

If you use a thermometer, push it into thickest part of the inside of the thigh muscle. Make sure the thermometer does not touch bone. When roasting a stuffed turkey, place bulb of thermometer in center of stuffing. The fowl will be done when temperature reaches 165°.

When testing for doneness, make the pinch test. Protect your thumb and forefinger with cloth or paper towel. Pinch the thickest of inside thigh muscle, being careful not to touch bone. When meat is done, it will seem very soft, and you can move the thigh up and down easily. The temperature should reach 165°, if you don't stuff the bird, which I prefer not to do.

To cook in open pan, rub with salt in cavity. My mother rubbed the skin with lard, but now you would rub with shortening. Do not cover pan or add water. Fold the wings under the fowl. Place on back. This will allow the juices from the back to go to the white meat that is dryer than the back. Start the fowl at about 420° for about 30 minutes and reduce to 300°. Add foil to cover top. Lift foil to baste occasionally. There will be drippings in bottom of pan for dressing and gravy. Buy canned broth if you need more. Turn up temperature the last 30 minutes if you need to brown on the bottom more. The modern way is to cook the turkey in a cooking bag, and that's what I prefer.

## Chicken

Just over a generation ago, chicken was so scarce and expensive that it was strictly reserved for Sunday dinner. Then the season determined what type chicken we would have for dinner. In the Spring we could only have fryers, in the Summer we could have the heavier fouls, and in the Fall we could have roasting hens and stewing chickens. Today, thanks to American know-how, all that has changed. No longer do I have to kill and dress that chicken – just go to the market and buy the fowl I want. I can buy wings, white meat, liver and gizzards, or drumsticks. Today, thanks to improved farming and production methods, chicken has turned out to be the best meat buy on the market, cheaper than beef, pork or lamb. As for food value, it is loaded with easily assimilated proteins and is probably the most easily digested food for both young and old alike.

# MRS. MILLS' ROAST TURKEY AND DRESSING

Before placing on a rack in an open roaster, cover the turkey with a paste. Cream together ¼ cup of soft butter (not melted), 5 Tbsp. of flour and 2 Tbsp. of lemon juice. This will look like whipped cream. Put heavy coating of this paste over the wings, breast and thigh joints. Also put a thin coating over the rest of the body. This will allow the turkey to brown nicely and be tender and moist.

DRESSING – This recipe makes a lot, so you can freeze some.

6 cups corn bread
4 cups stale white bread
> I use hamburger buns left out for a day to dry.

1½ cups celery (chopped)
1½ cups onions (chopped)
1 tsp. thyme
4 Tbsp. sage
4 eggs (beaten)
1 cup butter or Oleo (melted)
pepper to taste

Steam onions and celery in butter in iron skillet. Do not brown. Crumble the bread mixture into bite sizes. Mix the bread crumbs with the seasoning and set overnight. Next morning, steam celery and onions and add to bread mixture. Add a small amount of hot broth to moisten, then add melted butter and beaten eggs. Add more hot broth; just enough to make a dressing that will hold together. Press a handful of mixture into a ball that will hold together in your hand, but will break apart as it falls onto a plate. Then I know it has enough moisture to bake. Let it stand a few minutes. Add more broth if you think it needs it. Put in pan, well-greased, bake at 375° until done. Don't overcook.

GIBLET GRAVY

Pour off all fat from roast. Measure 4 Tbsp. of fat and return to roaster. Add 4 Tbsp. of flour which has been made into paste by adding a little cold water. Cook and brown well. Scrape all crustiness from sides of roaster. Cook flour well, but do not scorch. Use low heat. Add 2 cups of turkey broth. If you don't have 2 cups, finish with water. Cook until smooth and thickened. Add chopped liver and gizzard. Some like chopped hard-cooked eggs. By this time you may want to take a short-cut and use a can of cream of chicken soup diluted with a little milk. It makes a good gravy. You can add the giblets now.

# STEWED CHICKEN WITH OLD TIMEY ROLLED DUMPLINGS

1 stewing hen
3 tsp. salt or less
pepper to taste
(You want plenty of broth)

Place hen in deep kettle. Cover with water. Add 3 tsp. of salt and pepper to taste. Bring to boil. Reduce heat, cover tightly. Simmer for at least 2 hours, or until hen is real tender. Hen could be cooked in pressure cooker if you are pressed for time. I prefer the simmer process. Remove chicken from broth and cool. Remove chicken from bones and chop. If the hen is real fat, refrigerate and take off surplus fat.

DUMPLINGS (rolled):

2 cups all purpose flour
2 Tbsp. lard
1 egg (beaten in 3/4 cup milk)
½ tsp. salt

Put salt and flour in mixing bowl, add shortening and blend as for biscuit dough. When mixed, add beaten egg and milk mixture, gradually, until it forms a real stiff dough. Divide into 3 parts, roll each part very thin on a heavily floured board. Cut into strips about 2½ inches wide and 2-3 inches long. When all have been cut, drop one at a time into briskly boiling broth. Have liquid boiling all the time while dropping in dough strips. Boil for 10 minutes or longer, depending how tender you like them. Stir constantly to keep from sticking. If you need a richer broth, add bouillon cubes or cream of chicken soup. You haven't lived until you have eaten these old timey rolled dumplings.

This is a third generation recipe given to me by Helen Sloan Peyton. It is her mother's, Evie Clinkscale.

## DUMPLINGS
### Evie Clinkscale

½ cup sour milk
¼ tsp. soda
1 Tbsp. lard or shortening
1 tsp. salt
pepper to taste
flour

Add flour to make a soft dough. Roll thin and cut into long strips about 1" and then cut in squares. These dumplings can be used in short ribs (beef), spare ribs or chicken.

When Tom Allen, a brother-in-law, owned a family-style cafe during The Depression and World War II, he made dumplings with short ribs. They were mighty good then and would be now.

# BUTTERMILK FRIED CHICKEN

2 fryers 1½ lbs. each
2 cups flour (all purpose)
1½ tsp. baking powder
1½ tsp. baking soda
½ tsp. salt
¼ tsp. black pepper
3 cups buttermilk
fat for deep fat frying

Cut the chicken in serving pieces if not already cut up. Put 2 cups flour in paper bag, then shake 2 pieces at a time until all have been covered with flour. Add the baking powder, baking soda, salt and pepper to the rest of the flour in sack. Shake well to make sure the flour is well mixed. Dip each piece in buttermilk and then in flour mixture in sack. Shake well so that the chicken is completely covered with the flour mixture. An electric skillet is a great way to fry chicken. Set at 350° and fry until golden brown. Fry until well done, it will be golden brown

"A good name is rather to be chosen than great riches,
and loving favor rather than silver and gold."
Proverbs 22:1

# SMOTHERED CHICKEN

1 young hen (cut as for frying)
¼ cup lemon juice
½ cup flour
1 tsp. salt
pepper to taste
paprika to taste
1 cup fat (or use ½ shortening
      and ½ butter)
1 Tbsp. onion (minced)
2 Tbsp. parsley (chopped)
¼ clove of garlic
1½-2 cups sour cream

Rub chicken with lemon juice. Add salt, pepper, paprika to flour and coat each piece of chicken with flour, real heavily. Place in heated fat in heavy skillet, like a dutch oven, An electric skillet that's in just about every kitchen would be great now. Brown quickly on both sides. Sprinkle onion, garlic and parsley over top. Heat cream and add. Cover tightly, bake in 350° oven for 2½-3 hours. Serve on a bed of fluffy white rice. Fit for a king, but don't call the King, call me.

# SOUTHERN FRIED CHICKEN

Buy the size chicken
to fit needs
1½ cups flour (add more if
necessary)
2 eggs (beaten to a lemon
color)
1 cup milk
½ tsp. salt
¼ tsp. pepper
½ cup butter or corn oil
(My husband, Marvin, fried good
chicken, and he would use at least
a cup – half margarine and half oil.)

Dry the chicken pieces with paper towel (one at a time). Sprinkle lightly with a small part of the flour, set aside. Mix the eggs and milk together. Add the salt and pepper. Dip each piece into egg and milk mixture, then into flour. Coat well on all sides. Heat the oil in a large heavy hot skillet and brown each piece evenly on all sides. Reduce heat to very low, cover and cook for 30 minutes or until the thickest part tests done. If you like your chicken crisp and Southern Fried Chicken is supposed to be crisp, remove the cover and raise the heat some, if won't brown too much. Cook 5 minutes on 1 side, turn and cook 5 minutes on other side. Serve with gravy.

A thing of beauty is a joy forever. The gift without the giver is bare.

# CHICKEN GRAVY

The rule of thumb for gravy is 1 Tbsp. of drippings to 1 Tbsp. of flour (all purpose) and enough milk to thicken as you like.

3 heaping Tbsp. flour
½ tsp. salt
¼ tsp. pepper
1½ cups half and half
(To lower calories, I use dry milk, and if it gets thicker than I want, I thin with water. It's still good.)

Leave 3 Tbsp. of drippings in skillet. For easy mixing I use another Tbsp. of grease. Add flour, salt and pepper to drippings. Leave in skillet. Lower heat and cook until it bubbles and begins to brown slightly. Stir in cream and cook slowly, stirring constantly until the mixture is thickened. If too thick, add water. Much of the time it's poured over the chicken, but I prefer it served from a bowl and pour it over hot biscuits. If you're too tired, it's not bad over a slice of bread.

There are too many people who live without working and far too many that work without living.

Diogenes
a Cynic philosopher whose works flourished between 212-235 A.D.

This is another one of Gladys Puckett Moreau's delicious recipes.

## OVEN CHICKEN SALAD
Gladys Puckett Moreau

2 cups of cubed cooked
    chicken
2 cups celery (thinly sliced)
2 Tbsp. onion (grated)
1 cup real mayonnaise
½ tsp. salt
2 Tbsp. lemon juice
½ cup almonds (slivered)
1 cup bread crumbs (toasted)
½ cup cheese (grated)
1 cup potato chips (crushed)

Combine all ingredients except bread crumbs, potato chips and cheese. Pile lightly in a baking dish that has been sprayed with PAM. Sprinkle with grated cheese, bread crumbs and crushed potato chips mixed together. Bake at 450° for 15 minutes or until bubbly. Can be made ahead of time.

Toy Stove
photograph by Michael Allen

22

# CHICKEN AND RICE
Olevia Robinson

2 – 3 lb. fryers (cut up)
1 can cream of chicken soup
1 can cream of mushroom
     soup
1 can cream of celery soup
1 cup milk
1 cup uncooked rice

Mix together soups, milk and rice. Spread in bottom of 13"x9" baking dish. Place best of chicken on top. Bake uncovered for 3 hours at 300°.

Sandra Perkins' Federated Women's Club (Altruistic Club) in Carlisle, Arkansas had a Tastee. In preparation she looked in many cookbooks and found this recipe in a 1892 cookbook.

# WILD DUCK
Sandra Perkins
Carlisle, Arkansas

Fill pan with enough water to cover wild duck. Add chopped onion, apple, celery, pepper, and a little garlic. Top with 2 cans of sauerkraut. Cook all day.

My mother-in-law, Lou Allen, had twin sons, Floyd and Lloyd, and they loved to hunt and would bring home those wild ducks.

## LOU ALLEN'S WILD DUCK

Lou would boil them with an apple and onion, cut like to fry. After boiling she would take pieces from water, roll in a flour batter and fry for about an hour. Then she would add cream or milk and cook like smothered chicken. It was mighty good. She used lots of pepper and salt to taste. I would say this recipe is very creative. I've never seen a recipe like this.

**Eddie and Lou Allen**

**KITCHEN KAPERS:** When recipe calls for heavy cream, use ¾ cup of milk and ⅓ cup of vegetable oil.

24

# The Meat Industry

The meat industry has made a terrific change since the advent of refrigeration with big cattle trucks to get them to the stock yards and packing houses and refrigerated trucks to get them to the grocer in good shape. The pork and poultry industry have made the same changes.

The only beef we could have in the pioneer days was when somebody would kill a beef and "peddle" it out in the community. It was great to have a change from chicken and pork products. We hoped that somebody would come by when Grandmother Rogers would come in the Summer. I'm sure she missed the fresh meat, because Grandfather had a butcher shop in his general mercantile store in the Hill Country of South Texas. This was in the teens or early twenties. Grandfather died just before Christmas in a Brady, Texas, hospital in 1922.

## THE BEST EVER ROAST

5-7 lbs. of beef rump
    my favorite cut for roast
¾-1 lb. ham from ham hock
marinade – 3 parts oil to 1 part
    vinegar
1 clove of garlic
½ cup beef stock or ½ cup
    water with bullion cube
½ cup catsup
1 carrot (sliced)
few celery leaves

Trim fat from roast. Cut ham into strips
1½" long. Gash meat and insert ham

strips. Part of the ham will protrude, giving the meat a burry appearance. Marinate in vinegar and oil at least an hour. Turn several times. Use suet that you trim from the roast to rub the roaster with and heat real hot. Sear meat on all sides. Add hot stock mixed with catsup, celery leaves and sliced carrot. Cover with tight lid. Bake in a moderate oven at 325° and allow 35 minutes per pound, This is a delicious meat to slice and serve. For a perfect sandwich, try with rye bread. This is a top dollar meat, but think what you can do with it. Why not serve with parsley potatoes, fresh broccoli, a Jell-O salad or toss salad, whole wheat rolls, and Apple Brown Betty for dessert. You'll be the perfect hostess; I'll guarantee it!

## ROLLED ROAST
my second choice for roast

Buy about a 3½ lb. Pike's Peak Roast. You may have to ask your butcher to cut it for you. Place in shallow baking pan. Put in 400° oven uncovered, add no liquid. Allow 20-28 minutes per pound for roasting time. Salt when half done. Salt added in beginning tends to toughen the meat. This is also true with most vegetables.

The cheaper cuts of meat need to be cooked longer with liquid and cover.

# POT ROAST

4-5 lbs. pot roast (round, chuck or shoulder)
2 Tbsp. oil
1 cup of dry red wine
  for wine substitute use ½ cup water, ½ cup vinegar and 2 tsp. sugar
2 pieces of orange peel 2"x2"
  just the orange part, omit the white
2 cinnamon sticks (3 inches)
12 small onions (peeled)
1 cup tomato sauce
5 whole cloves
1 clove of garlic

Heat oil in a large dutch own. Add roast and brown on all sides. Add tomato sauce, wine, orange peel, cloves, cinnamon, and garlic. Cover and bake 300° for 3 hours. Now add onions. Cook 1 hour longer or until tender. It'll be much easier sliced if let set for 15 minutes. Always cut across the grain.

The world needs inspiration just as much as information.

# BARBEQUED BEEF
using left over roast

Cut left over roast into slices. Place in shallow pan, do not pack. Brush generously with barbeque sauce. Turn once. Baste or brush often with sauce. Maybe grilled or cooked in hot oven. Use this sauce.

# BARBEQUE SAUCE
very simple

1 Tbsp. butter
2 thin slices onion
       (medium size)
½ tsp. pepper
1 Tbsp. sugar
1 tsp. mustard
1 tsp. paprika
¼ cup tomato catsup
¼ cup vinegar
¾ cup water

Melt butter and saute´ onion in it until a pale yellow. Add dry seasonings, catsup, vinegar, and water. Bring to a boiling point. Use for brushing or basting sauce.

# BARBECUED SHORT RIBS
## OF BEEF

2½-3 lbs. beef short ribs
1 large onion (sliced)
½ cup catsup
½ cup vinegar
2 tsp. chili powder
1 tsp. paprika
2½ tsp. salt

Cut ribs in individual servings. Brown in hot fat in heavy skillet. Place in baking dish. Slice onion over top. Mix together the catsup, vinegar, chili powder, paprika, and salt. Pour over ribs. Bake in slow oven 325° for 1½ hours or until tender.

# BARB-Q MEATBALLS
Leonore Cruzan
Bartlesville, OK

1 lb. ground meat
½ cup bread crumbs
1 egg (slightly beaten)
salt and pepper to taste

Combine mixture and roll in 1" balls. Bake in 350° oven for 45 minutes. Pour off extra fat. Cover with Barb-Q Sauce, then bake 20 minutes longer.

Combine the following:
½ cup catsup
¼ cup onions
2 tsp. vinegar
2 tsp. Worcestershire sauce
½ cup water
6 drops of liquid smoke
salt and pepper to taste

Cover meatballs with this mixture and cook in electric skillet or a large one or can cook in oven.

**KITCHEN KAPERS:** To stretch hamburger, add a grated potato or dry cereal. Oatmeal is good.

I've never heard of tomato gravy and began having calls for it. I finally found this recipe from a Searchlight Recipe Book, copyright dated 1931.

# MEATBALLS
# AND
# TOMATO GRAVY

1 lb. lean ground beef
¼ lb. pork sausage
2 Tbsp. onions (chopped)
1 cup soft bread crumbs
cayenne pepper
paprika
1 clove of garlic (chopped)
2 eggs (well beaten)
4 cups tomato juice
½ tsp. nutmeg
salt and pepper to taste

Combine sausage and meat. Add nutmeg, bread crumbs, onion, garlic, eggs, and a few grains of cayenne pepper and paprika. Season to taste. Form in small balls. Roll in flour. Heat tomato juice to boiling. Drop meatballs into boiling juice. Cover and simmer 40 minutes. To simmer means just barely bubbling. The juices from the meat, thickened with bread will make its own sauce.

# CHILI CON CARNE
in memory of Floyd Robinson

2 lbs. ground chili meat
3 Tbsp. chili powder
3 Tbsp. flour
1 tsp. black pepper
2 tsp. salt
1 tsp. cumin seed or powder
2 Tbsp. fat
5 or 6 dashes Tabasco sauce
3 cups water

Brown meat lightly, add chili powder, mixed with flour, salt and pepper, and cumin seed or powder. Cook until well browned; add water and cook until well done, then add 2 cans of pinto or brown beans. We prefer the Ellis brand of pinto beans. Serves 8.

# CALLENE'S CHILI
Callene Crockwell
Dover, TN

2 lbs. of ground chuck
2 medium onions (chopped)
1 can red kidney beans
2 cans Mexican chili beans
        (Bush brand)
1 quart canned tomatoes
chili powder to taste
(McCormick brand)
salt to taste

Simmer 1½ hours. Callene says this is the best ever.

# CHICKEN FRIED STEAK

2 lbs. round steak cutlets
    (tenderized)
1-2 cups flour
1½ tsp. salt
1 tsp. pepper
½ cup milk
1 egg
oil

Have about 2" of oil in heavy skillet. Blend egg and milk together. Combine flour with salt and pepper. Dip meat into egg mixture, then force as much flour as possible into the steak. In other words, coat well. Put meat into hot grease and cook 3-4 minutes, turn and cook for the same time on other side. Only turn once. To keep the coating on good, you need to start in very hot grease, then lower heat. To crisp it, if desired, raise heat before taking from skillet.

## SWISS STEAK

1½ cups flour
1 tsp. salt
½ tsp. pepper
3 lbs. of round steak
    You probably will have to get your
    butcher to cut this.
1½" thick suet or 3 Tbsp. fat

1 can whole tomatoes
     (sieved)
6 carrots (peeled or scraped)
9 onions (small)

Mix the flour and salt and pepper together. Cover 1 side of the meat with the flour mixture. With a heavy-edged saucer, pound the seasoned flour into 1 side of the meat. Turn and generously pound the other side. Repeat until all seasoned flour has been pounded into the steak. This part is tedious, but is necessary. In electric skillet or heavy fry pan, fry out the suit. Brown all the meat on both sides in the hot fat. Add the sieved tomatoes. Cover the lid tightly and simmer 1½ hour or until tender. During the last 30 minutes of cooking, add carrots and onions. Chopped celery could also be added. Serve from skillet.

# STEAK SAN MARCO

Helen Keener
Oklahoma City

2 lbs. chuck steak (1" thick, cut
    into serving pieces)
1 envelope Lipton Onion
    Soup Mix
1 can or 1 lb. Italian peeled
    tomatoes
1 tsp. oregano
freshly ground pepper and
garlic powder to taste
2 Tbsp. cooking oil
2 Tbsp. wine vinegar

In large skillet (I use my electric skillet), arrange meat, cover with onion soup and tomatoes, sprinkle with oregano, garlic powder, pepper, oil, and vinegar. Simmer covered for 1½ hours, or until meat is tender. Easy and good. Serves 6.

# STEAK TIPS IN BROWN GRAVY

Eunice Talley

1 lb. round steak cut in thin finger strips or sirloin tips. Salt, pepper and flour the strips, then brown in oil, remove strips and add 2 Tbsp. flour to drippings and still well. Add the following: 2 cups beef bouillon, 1 tsp. kitchen bouquet, 1 tsp. brown sugar, 1 tsp. mustard. Put strips back in gravy and simmer for 20-30 minutes, covered.

People who don't care for meat loaf will like this one.

# MEAT LOAF

1½ lbs. lean ground meat
1 cup uncooked oatmeal
2 eggs (beaten)
2 Tbsp. brown sugar
1½ tsp. salt
½ tsp. pepper
4 oz. tomato sauce

Mix all the ingredients and form in a loaf pan. Bake 350° for 15 minutes. In the meantime prepare the sauce.

Sauce:
4 oz. tomato sauce
2 Tbsp. vinegar
2 Tbsp. prepared mustard

Mix all ingredients for sauce and pour over meat. Continue to bake for another hour. Baste 2-3 times with sauce. Serve with cream pota-toes or noodles or serve on a nest of fluffy rice.

There are but two objects in marriage – love and money. If you marry for love, you will certainly have many happy days and a few uneasy ones. If you marry for money, you may have many easy days, but few happy ones.
Lord Chesterfield

# STUFFED PEPPER
Olevia Robinson

4 large green peppers
1 lb. lean ground beef
1 small onion (chopped)
2 cups rice (cooked)
1- 8 oz. can of tomato sauce
2 Tbsp. celery (chopped)
1 tsp. salt
a dash of pepper

Cut thin slice from stem end of pepper, remove seeds with tsp., discard. Combine onion and chopped beef in skillet. Add remaining ingredients except peppers, mix well. Stuff peppers with mixture and place in baking dish, cover and bake at 350° for 45 minutes.

# STUFFED BEEF HEART

This is very good and really neglected. Buy a dark red beef heart. It will weigh about 2 lbs. Carefully feel for the gristle that support the cavities. Use sharp paring knife to remove all the gristle. Pat dry with paper towel.

Now for your stuffing:
¼ cup fine bread crumbs
2 Tbsp. onions (minced)
1 tsp. parsley (minced)
½ cup cooked rice

1 stalk celery (chopped)
1 bay leaf
1 Tbsp. crisp bacon (minced)
½ cup hot stock
      (bullion cube)

Fill cavity of heart with stuffing. Don't pack. Wrap with cord. Use 2 long skewers across top to hold. Dust heart with salt and pepper. Heat ¼ cup shortening in heavy roaster. While shortening is getting hot, coat with flour. Sear all the way around. Add stock. Cover with a tight lid. Cook about 1½ hours in 350° oven. Serve in bed of fluffy rice. Drizzle some of the rich gravy over heart. Always slice meat across grain.Stuffing is used mostly to season the heart.

Debbie Taylor says this recipe came from her husband's father. Debbie has used it for over 50 years, and her husband vows it's the best.

## SOUTHERN HASH
in memory of Rev. Floyd Taylor

½ lb. ground pork
½ lb. ground beef
7-8 Irish potatoes (diced)
5 onions (diced)
½ tsp. poultry seasoning
5 cups catsup
salt and pepper to taste

Cook until done. Serve on rice.

## Just Luck, I Guess

When I married you,
I never asked if you
could balance a checkbook
or iron a shirt,
or if you wanted
one baby or six.
We set sail
on waters unknown
and did quite well
at filling our log
with notations of bliss.
I never dreamed
I was getting a woman
who know 46 ways
to cook hamburger.

L. G. Harvey
From "Yes, Ann Landers, I Would Do It Again."

There is one thing more exasperating
than a wife who can cook and won't,
and that is the wife who can't cook and will.
Robert Frost

To live life fully,
we must learn to
love people and use things!
Not love things
and use people!

# FISH

# Fishing In The Past

Fishing is not my favorite meat, but fishing was a favorite pastime when I was a kid. The only fresh fish we had then was caught in the creek with a hook and line. Then there was the fear of swallowing a bone.

When the water got warm enough in the Summer, we would make a picnic out of seining from a pretty big creek not far from where we lived. There were several families that joined us in this exciting adventure. We'd all pile in our wagons about the middle of the afternoon with all the makings of a fish fry, like grease, fresh onions and meal. For bread, corn bread was fried in a skillet. We would sleep in the wagon and go home in the middle of the next day in order to get ready for church on Sunday.

The children were allowed to bathe in the creek. One mother was assigned the job of watching us for fear we'd slip off in a big hole in the bed of the creek. The water was never over our heads. I don't remember anyone ever doing that. It was fun for the whole family until somebody passed a law saying we couldn't seine anymore.

Then we went to putting out trotlines, a sport only enjoyed by the men, done at night by the light of the moon or those kerosene lanterns.

Fishing has become so sophisticated today. In the past when friends would ask me to go fishing with them, my reply was, "Thanks, but no thanks. If that was all I had to do, I'd commit suicide." They don't ask me anymore; I wonder why? Could it be because I'm 83 years old?

# HINTS ON FRYING FISH

Always have fat hot whether lard, butter or vegetable oil and have plenty of it. Soak fish 15-20 minutes in cold water. It should be drained and all moisture absorbed with a paper towel.

## BAKED FISH

Mlx:
1 tsp. celery salt
a dash of garlic powder
1 tsp. Worcestershire sauce
salt and pepper to taste
juice of 1 lemon

Melt ½ cup butter, spoon over top of fish. Sprinkle sauce over all fish rolled in cracker crumbs, meal or crushed almonds. Arrange fish on a cookie sheet and bake at 375°, or until meat is flaky and a crusty brown. If need to brown more, you can raise the heat. Most people would say garnish with thin lemon slices and serve with tartar sauce, hush puppies, cabbage slaw, and French fries.

**KITCHEN KAPERS:** When baking fish, put on a bed of chopped celery, onions and parsley. It not only will improve the taste, but it will keep it from sticking.

# SEAFOOD CASSEROLE

3 hard cooked eggs (sliced)
1 can (5 oz.) of shrimp (cut)
1 can (5 oz.) of tuna
1 can (2 oz.) mushrooms
1 can (6½ oz.) crabmeat
2 cups medium white sauce
¼ lb. cheddar cheese
    (grated)
¼ lb. butter (melted)
1 cup bread crumbs

Put layers of egg, shrimp, tuna, crab-meat, and mushrooms in a buttered casserole, pouring cream sauce over each layer. Sprinkle top with cheese and buttered bread crumbs. Bake at 350° for 45 minutes.

This recipe was used when we had a 15¢ can of salmon. Fifteen cents would buy the best: Red Sock Eye. This recipe was done before the Depression and was a treat then. Salmon was considered a poor man's meat during The Depression. We might put it outside to mold and chill in order to slice.

# MOCK FISH

Mush with:
3 cups water
¾ cup cornmeal
1 scant tsp. salt

Stir slowly the cornmeal into the boiling water, stirring constantly. Add salt and cook until real thick. When the mush has cooled, add a can of salmon. Roll in meal and fry in hot fat. As my little cousin, J. M. Bonds would say, "Iss tastes iss like fish."

## SALMON LOAF

1 can (15 oz.) salmon
1⅓ cups cheese of your choice
        (grated)
1½ cup evaporated milk or milk
½ tsp. salt
1 egg (beaten)
1 cup bread crumbs (coarse)
3 Tbsp. Oleo (melted)
1 Tbsp. lemon juice
⅛ tsp. black pepper
a pinch of cayenne pepper

Put salmon in mixing bowl, remove bone and skin, flake and mix with the rest of the ingredients and put in a well-greased baking dish. Bake at 350° for about 30-40 minutes.

# SALMON CROQUETTES
Jeannette Weaver

1 extra large potato (cooked, peeled and mashed)
1 large can of Pacific salmon (red or pink)
½ pkg. Goodseasoning salad dressing mix (Italian)
1 large egg or 2 regular eggs (beaten)
½-1 fresh lemon (juice)
cornmeal crackers (crushed)

Mix all ingredients except cornmeal and crackers. Set in refrigerator 3-4 hours to season. Add crackers and shape into patties. Roll in cornmeal. Fry in hot Crisco or vegetable oil. Serve warm.

# SWEET AND SOUR FISH

2 lbs. of sole or halibut fillets (cut into 1" cubes)
salad oil to brown fish
medium onion (chopped)
1 medium green pepper (chopped)
1 clove of garlic (minced)
1 large tomato (cut in cubes)

Roll fish in cornstarch; shake off excess. Brown on all sides with a little vegetable oil. Drain. Then in another pan, heat 2 Tbsp. oil over high heat. Add garlic, onion and pepper; cook while stirring for 2 minutes. Add sweet and sour sauce. Heat and stir until sauce thickens for 1 minute. Add tomato cubes and pour over fish. Why not serve on a bed of white fluffy rice? I like to prepare sweet and sour sauce first.

Sweet and sour sauce:

1 Tbsp. cornstarch
¼ cup sugar
2 Tbsp. soy sauce
2 Tbsp. catsup
¼ cup vinegar
½ cup chicken broth (can use chicken bullion cube)

Mix cornstarch with sugar and pour in the rest of the ingredients.

# SOUR CREAM SOLE FILLET

1½ lbs. of fillets of your choice
     (halibut can be used)
1 cube of butter or Oleo
     (melted)
salt and pepper to taste
 paprika
1 pkg. sliced almonds 1 cup
sour cream

Rinse fish and pat dry with paper towel. Dip in butter. Sprinkle both sides with salt, pepper and paprika. Place in baking dish. Bake in 350° oven for about 30 minutes or until fish is flaky. Drain butter and leave a little to cover bottom of dish. Spread sour cream over the fish, completely cover. Spread cheese over the sour cream and top with almonds. Return to oven for 10-15 minutes, or until cheese is melted. Menu suggestion: garlic French bread, tossed green salad and maybe a gelatin salad for dessert. Just a plain fruit salad would be good.

# TUNA CASSEROLE
Olevia Robinson

2 cans (7 oz.) tuna (drained
    and flaked)
½ cup milk
2 cups noodles (cooked)
1 cup cooked peas
1 Tbsp. pimento
1 Tbsp. butter
2 Tbsp. bread crumbs ( or
    potato chips crushed)
1 can celery soup

Combine soup and milk. Stir in noodles, peas, pimento, and tuna. Cover and bake at 400° oven for 25 minutes. Top with buttered crumbs or potato chips. Bake for 5 minutes more. In hot butter stir in bread crumbs until lightly browned.

# HOW TO BOIL CATFISH
Joyce Allen
Salisbury, NC

Cook catfish in very little water with onion for about 10 minutes or until tender. Peel off skin when cool enough to handle. Use like tuna fish. Now we can have fish anytime – fresh or canned.

# BATTERED CATFISH

1-2 lbs. of fish fillets
1 cup shortening
1 cup butter

Melt in medium frying pan real hot the butter and shortening.

Mix:
½ cup milk
1 egg
½-1 cup cornmeal
salt and pepper to taste

Drop fillets in milk mixture. Roll in meal and drop in the hot grease. Watch closely; it will brown quickly. Fry about 7 minutes. Turn once. This can be baked in the oven. Prepare with batter as to fry, but put in a shallow pan in oven. Bake 400° until the fish is brown. Then turn and brown the other side. Before putting in oven, drizzle top with Oleo.

# FRUITS
## AND
## VEGETABLES

# Fresh Vegetables

We used lots of onions in the Pioneer Days in just about every conceivable way. We started using them early when they were barely big enough to pull. They were baked with the blades in corn bread and put into mush that we usually had for supper. It was so good cooked with the blades, seasoned with butter, salt and pepper. The onions never failed us. They came in too early for the hot weather to damage them, and if they were in a hail storm, they came back up – not so with other vegetables. The onion in the corn bread and mush was a change from the plain bread and mush we had throughout the winter months. We boiled the medium size onions. They were drained and seasoned with butter, salt and pepper.

Most of the onions were left in the ground to make bigger ones. When they were ready to harvest, they were pulled up, tied in bundles and hung in the smokehouse with the blades down to dry out. We used lots of winter onions in soups, stews, corn bread stuffing, and fall greens. We had to get a start of onions from somebody. They were always there when we needed them. When pulled, they would make room to multiply. They never had to be watered and never froze – rain or shine, sleet or snow. They were green when everything else was dead. I can still see them just behind the smokehouse.

When the regular onions were gone, all my mother had to say was, "One of you get me some onions." We knew to go right then. My sister and I usually went. We did most everything together from making beds to gathering eggs. It was more fun and quicker.

We gathered the vegetables in the early morning before the dew was gone. They were fresher then, and besides it was very hot up in the day. It was hot in the house, too, with no fans. All we could do was open windows and doors to create a draft. We looked forward to the fresh vegetables, and compared to now we don't know what fresh is.

This recipe was given to me by Mary Jo Flatt of Mt. Juliet, Tennessee. It was created by her father, Charlie Durham. During the summer his pleasure in growing yellow squash often outweighed his pleasure in eating them. He came up with this recipe, which has for years been a favorite with their family. It can easily be adjusted to cooking any quantity desired.

## FRIED SQUASH WITH POTATOES
### Charlie Durham

Cut up equal amounts of yellow squash and white potatoes. Add chopped onion to your taste. Pour enough buttermilk over the mixture to lightly coat. Then roll in cornmeal.

In a skillet pour enough vegetable oil (2-3 Tbsp.) to cover the surface and let it get hot. Add the mixture to the skillet and reduce the heat to simmer. Salt and pepper to taste. Cover with a lid and let cook until potatoes are tender and mixture is brown on the bottom.

Flip all the mixture over, turn the heat up to medium, leave lid off and brown the underneath side. Continue to cook and stir occasionally until it becomes as brown as you like. Serve hot. Bacon drippings can be used in the place of the oil and will add to the flavor.

Black eyed peas were imported from Nigeria. They were a staple in Southern states and eventually became a tradition with the white people. We eat them for good luck on New Year's Day.

## BLACK-EYED PEAS

2 cups dried black-eyed peas
6½ cups water

Pick over peas and remove any broken peas. Wash well. Soak overnight in 2 cups water. Let them come to a good rolling boil. Remove from fire and set for 1 hour covered. Drain off water. Add the 6½ cups water and let come to rolling boil and then simmer until done. About 20 minutes before they are done, add 1 lb. of any good sausage made into balls about walnut size. Serve with hot buttered corn bread and cabbage slaw. Real good "eatin'" and very nutritious. Real good warmed over. A sweet sliced onion on top improves it, if available. I cook pinto beans the same way.

**KITCHEN KAPERS:** When frying okra, cut the stems off; when boiling okra, leave a short stem. This keeps it from becoming so slick.

This recipe was given to me by Judy Everett and is favorite of all the kids and grandchildren. Judy is originally from Duncan, Oklahoma, and still has family there.

## OKRA PATTIES
in memory of Emily Mary Townsend

1½ cups sliced okra
2 Tbsp. buttermilk
3 Tbsp. flour
2 Tbsp. cornmeal
salt and pepper
1 egg (beaten)
cooking oil (small amount)

Boil okra in small amount of water until soft and tender. Drain well. Combine in bowl flour, cornmeal, egg, salt and pepper, and buttermilk. Stir in boiled okra. Mix well. Drop by Tbsp. into hot skillet with heated oil. Fry until brown.

## FRIED GREEN TOMATOES

Select round, green and firm tomatoes of average size just before they begin to turn. Slice about ¼" thick and soak in salt water before frying. Dip in a mixture of ½ cup meal and ½ cup flour to turn in. The flour will make it cling to the tomato slices. Fry until a deep brown in hot lard. When we made a good crop, this enabled us to put another dish on the table before they got ripe. If preferred, you could scald the tomatoes with boiling water to peel before slicing.

# AUNT LELA'S CORN CUSTARD

2 cups corn cut from cob
or
1 can corn
2 cups milk
2 Tbsp. flour (mixed with a little
        cold milk)
1 Tbsp. butter
½ tsp. salt
2 Tbsp. sugar
1 egg (beaten)

Mix flour, salt, sugar, and add to a beaten egg. Mix thoroughly with corn and add to the hot milk. Pour in 1 quart baking pan. Dot with butter. Set in pan of hot water and bake until custard is set for about 1 hour at 325°.

## WILTED LETTUCE
Linda Morley
Victoria, Texas

Wash well and chop together, leaf lettuce, mustard greens and shellot onions. Pour over hot bacon grease. It was probably home-cured salt pork. Eat with onions and corn bread. This was eaten in the Spring.

The above recipe was made by Linda Morley's grandmother, passed on to her mother and then to Linda. Her mother and grandmother were born and reared in the hills of Arkansas and Mississippi.

Marilyn Gonsman makes this recipe for Thanksgiving and Christmas. She says it's a favorite of her kids. She also says, "This is to die for."

## ONION CELESTE
Marilyn Gonsman
Blairsville, GA

4-5 large yellow onions
(chopped)
2 Tbsp. Butter
½ lb. swiss cheese (shredded)
½ lb. parmesan cheese
(shredded)
¼ tsp. pepper
1 can cream of celery soup
¼ cup milk

Cook onions in butter until clear. Pour into greased baking dish. Spread swiss cheese on top of onion. Sprinkle with pepper. Heat soup and milk. Pour over onions, sprinkle with parmesan cheese. Cover with foil, refrigerate overnight. Bake 45 minutes covered, then remove cover and let brown.

**KITCHEN KAPERS:** When mashing potatoes, add ¼ level tsp. of baking powder to 2 cups potatoes. This keeps potatoes fluffy even until the next day.

With so many working housewives, this is a dish you can prepare ahead of time or prepare quickly for dinner. Serve with hot buttered corn bread, and a side dish of chow-chow would be good! Top it with fruit salad.

## QUICK BAKED BUTTER BEANS

Open 1 or 2 cans of large butter beans. Drain and place in deep baking dish. Sprinkle with brown sugar and dot generously with butter. Lay strips of half cooked bacon on top. Add another layer of butter beans, sugar and butter. Top with strips of uncooked bacon. Bake in 350° oven for about 25 minutes.

## BAKED BEANS
### the modern way

2 large cans of pork and
    beans
¾ cup brown sugar
2 Tbsp. Worcestershire sauce
1 tsp. Tabasco sauce
1 medium onion
6 slices of crisp bacon
    (crumbled)
1 medium green pepper
    (chopped)
1 cup catsup (chopped)

Combined all ingredients, bake in 9"x13" flat pan in 300° oven for 3 hours. Stir occasionally. Serves 10-15. For a smaller amount, divide in half.

This recipe must have been cooked on a wood-burning stove when you put the pan on back of the stove to keep warm.

## HARVARD BEETS

Mix:
½ cup sugar
1 tsp. flour
½ tsp. salt
⅓ cup vinegar
⅓ cup boiling water

Cook until sauce is clear. Add 2 cups of freshly cooked beets, drained and diced. Keep beets and sauce in a warm place for 30 minutes. Add 2 Tbsp. butter and serve.

## YALE BEETS
(casserole)

1 can sliced beets

Place in baking dish and pour sauce over beets:
¼ cup sugar
2 tsp. flour
1 tsp. salt
½ cup orange juice
1 Tbsp. lemon juice
2 Tbsp. melted butter

Mix well and bake 25 minutes in 350° oven.

The definition of a Pioneer: A man who formerly blazed a trail whose decedents now burn up the road.

# SOUTHERN FRIED OKRA

1 lb. of fresh okra
1 tsp. salt
¼ tsp. pepper
1 egg (slightly beaten)
¼ cup flour
¾ cup meal

Wash and cut okra crosswise into ⅓"-½" pieces. Dredge in a mixture of flour and meal with salt and pepper, added, until well-coated. Stir egg in okra-flour mixture and put in a skillet with hot grease. Stir as needed, cover if like it soft; crisp it with the lid off. Okra is good served with fresh tomatoes. Corn bread just has to be a must.

Cabbage is the fastest growing vegetable in popularity. It's also appreciated for its nutritious value and can be bought the year 'round. For those who think they don't like cabbage are in for a surprise.

# CABBAGE WITH CHEESE SAUCE

1 head of cabbage, washed and grated. Steam in very little water for 10-15 minutes. Drain and put in a casserole and add this cheese sauce:

4-5 Tbsp. butter or margarine
1 cup milk
1 cup sharp cheese (grated)
2 Tbsp. flour
garlic salt to taste
salt and pepper to taste

Make cheese sauce from flour, milk, cheese and butter. Add salt, pepper, garlic salt. Bake 350° for 20-25 minutes.

# FIX AHEAD MASHED POTATOES
Marilyn Gonsman
Blairsville, GA

3 lbs. potatoes (do not use
   baking potatoes)
¾ tsp. salt
2 tsp. butter
2 - pkg. (3 oz.) cream cheese
¼ cup milk

Peel and cube potatoes until done with ¾ tsp. salt. Mash. Add 2 Tbsp. butter and next four ingredients, mixing until all are blended. Pour into a greased baking dish. Brush top with melted butter, sprinkle with bread crumbs, cheese and paprika. This can be made ahead and refrigerated. If refrigerated let stand 30 minutes before baking. Bake about 30 minutes at 350° or until brown.

I remember the lady who gave me this recipe, but somehow I lost her name. Sorry about that, and thanks for the recipe. She was very enthusiastic about it. She said it could be used as a side or main dish with polish sausage or any good brand in a casing.

## FRIED CABBAGE

Cut cabbage in half and then into wedges. Fry in bacon grease. Turn as you fry. When cabbage wilts, add sausage in bottom of skillet to brown. When cooked a short time, add ¼ - ⅓ cup of water. Add lid and cook just a few minutes. Do not overcook it.

# Fruits

We had very little fruit in the off season, just what we had canned or dried or had bought already dried. We had raisins, prunes, apricots, peaches, or apples. They were soaked in enough water to cover good overnight or 2-3 hours. They were cooked in the water they were soaked in. They were cooked until tender and sweetened to taste. This fruit was on the noon or supper table and eaten with hot bread. Sometimes they were eaten with oatmeal for breakfast or with rice for supper. They were also used to cook with, especially in cake.

In the early Fall there were apples and pears, and of course, there were peaches in the Summertime. The apples were not of good quality, but we did make apple butter, canned and used some for pies. When my grandmother came for a visit, she would help dry some apples. The canned peaches might be served with whipped cream. We didn't have to have cake or cookies to go with them. We thought they were good with cold biscuits

It seem we don't use the simple recipes as we did in the past. This one is simple.

## BAKED APPLES

Wash and core large green, sour apples. Fill apples with cinnamon, sugar and a small pat of butter. Put in a baking pan with enough water to cover bottom of pan. Keep covered until done in 350° oven. Variations: raisins and pat of butter, nuts and pecans and brown sugar.

Lost time is never found.

# FRIED APPLES

Fried apples were so good in the early Fall. I can still smell the aroma from the cinnamon. My mother would peel, cut out the wormy spots, core and cut in eights enough apples to fill a big skillet with ¼-½ cups of bacon grease with about ¼ cup butter. Reduce heat, cover and steam about 10 minutes. Then sprinkle with ¾ cup of white sugar or ¾ cup brown sugar. Add a little lemon juice or 1 Tbsp. vinegar. Cover and cook slowly, stirring to prevent sticking. Shake about 1 tsp. cinnamon and nutmeg when adding sugar. Add little water if needed and cook until tender. This recipe puts an extra delicious dish on the table.

## SCALLOPED APPLES

Peel, slice and core as many apples as needed. Place a layer of sliced apples in bottom of baking dish. Sprinkle wit sugar; dot with plenty of butter. Sprinkle with cinnamon. Put in another layer of apples, sugar and cinnamon. Press down. Repeat until dish is heaping full. Cover apples and cook 1-1½ hours at 300°. You might want to sprinkle bread crumbs over top and bake in 350° oven for 45 minutes with lid off.

This recipe was handwritten by Aunt Sue in her 1927 P.T.A. cookbook.

# CHEESE APPLE CRISP

4 cups apples (sliced and
     peeled)
1 tsp. lemon juice
½ tsp. cinnamon
¾ cup sugar
½ cup flour
⅜ cup water
⅛ tsp. salt
⅛ tsp. allspice
¼ cup butter
1 cup American cheese
     (grated)

Add lemon juice to water. Slice apples into water. Put apples into greased 6x10 inch baking dish. Pour lemon water over apples. Sprinkle with cinnamon and allspice. Combine sugar, flour and salt with fingers. Work in butter until mixture looks like crumbs. Lightly stir in cheese. Stir the mixture over apples. Bake at 350° for 30 minutes. Serve hot or cold with ice cream or whipped cream.

**KITCHEN KAPERS:** Submerge a lemon in hot water 15 minutes will increase the amount of juice by nearly half. 1 lemon will yield 3 tsp. of juice. 1 average lemon will yield 1 tbsp.. grated rind.

Mrs. Mammie Hickerson was a client of mine for nearly 50 years. She came to Altus, Oklahoma, in 1928 with her husband, Henry, and their only child, Harold, from Missouri and went into the furniture business in 1933. She lived to be 92½ and worked in the store 6 months prior to her death. Harold and his wife Katherine have 7 children, Mammie's pride and joy. When having a family dinner, Mrs. Hickerson would furnish the vegetables and was expected to bring those tasty stewed apples. The grandchildren just had to have those apples. Mr.s. Hickerson, a beautiful lady, adored by many, a favorite of mine, and missed by all who knew her. The store is still operated by the family.

## MRS. HICKERSON'S STEWED APPLES

Cook apples with very little sugar and not much water. Be stingy with the spices and do not overcook. The perfect meat accompaniment.

In the early days, if in deer country, venison was used for mincemeat. You can freeze it, can it or refrigerate it. The recipe will make 4 pies and can be used in cakes and cookies.

# MINCEMEAT

1 qt. cooked meat (chopped)
2 cups raisins
2 cups dried apricots
        (chopped)
2 qts. apples (chopped)
1 qt. cider or apple juice
4 lemons (use juice and
        grated rind)
4 tsp. salt
1 tsp. allspice
4 tsp. cinnamon
4 cups brown sugar
1 cup suet (chopped)

Mix all ingredients in a large heavy pan. It needs to be cooked for about 1¼ hours. Stir frequently. Pack into hot sterile jars and seal. If put in pies, see Marie Mills' instructions for Two Crust Pineapple Pie on page 118. Substitute mincemeat for pineapple. To freeze, have pie assembled ready to bake. Freeze in pie shell and remove the pie plate and put in ziplock bag. Always serve mince pie hot. Good for Christmas gift. Put in a little basket or create your own wrap.

To err is human; to forgive is divine.

# DESSERTS

# Aunt Sue

Many of the recipes in this book where my Aunt Sue's. One summer after my mother died, my sister and I spent the Summer with Aunt Sue and Uncle Ennis. She was the youngest in the family, and they were young enough to be a lot of fun. Uncle Ennis was fortunate enough to have a job all during The Depression. He was a mechanic for the International Harvester Company. This was a wheat growing country in the plains of Texas. My father worked in the harvest out in the country for a cousin, and Marie and I stayed in town with Aunt Sue and Uncle Ennis.

I recall before they left for home from my mother's funeral, Uncle Ennis sat down at the dining room table and wrote Marie and me a check for $5$\underline{^{00}}$ each. The first check we ever had. It bought us a pair of black patent leather shoes with cuban heels (a low blocky heel). To keep them pretty and shiny, we rubbed them with a cold biscuit. They were strickly "Sunday shoes."

Aunt Sue lived to be nearly 96. When she died I inherited all her recipes which I really treasure. I'm happy to pass them on to you. You'll love them, too. I have her bank deposit book that was dated May, 1920. Her first deposit was $5.00 – a high school graduation gift. She was the only one in my father's family to finish high school. My aunt didn't have many deposits in her book, because she soon married. The balance of her deposit book was filled with recipes. She married her high school sweetheart, Ennis McCollum. This was in Kimble County, Texas. This area of Texas is rich in pioneer history. Governor Coke Stephenson, Admiral David Nimitz of World War I fame and President Lyndon B. Johnson were from this area. My grandfather, Dense Rogers, purchased a general mercantile store in London and became the second owner. He and his wife, Ollie, lived above the store. The first owner sold supplies to the cowboys on the cattle drives that started in Texas and ended in Kansas at the railheads. Aunt Sue and Uncle Ennis soon moved to the Amarillo, Texas, area (Dimmet and Hereford). Later, they moved back to the London area. My father was a freight hauler in that area around 1919. There was no railroad in London so he hauled freight in a wagon from Menard to London . He couldn't make it in one day, so he had to camp out at night, sleep in the wagon and build a campfire to cook. Needless to say, he didn't work at this job very long.

### Thelma, Aunt Sue and Marie
November 29, 1991

### Dense Rogers' Store
Photograph courtesy of
Leroy R. Borden
(Leroy is Dense Rogers' grandson and my first cousin)

This recipe was passed down from Aunt Sue's mother, my grandmother Ollie. I have no way of knowing how old this recipe is. My grandmother was born in 1861. She was 61 when her husband, Dense Rogers (my grandfather) died. Her children thought she was too old to live alone and keep house. Now, she would tell her kids to "go fly a kite," and that she would manage the store and maintain her own home. She knew nothing of the business and had never worked outside the home.

This was a very popular cake in The Pioneer Days. It required no refrigeration. The fruit was available the "year-round" and was cheap. The ingredients were in everybody's kitchen. It was very popular with the "men folk," nothing fancy – just plain good.

## AUNT SUE'S
## STACKED DRIED APPLE CAKE
6 layers

1¾ cup granulated sugar
¼ cup molasses or brown sugar
1 scant cup of lard
        or 1 cup butter
2 eggs
½ cup buttermilk
6 cups flour
        (measured after sifting)
3 tsp. baking powder
1 scant tsp. soda
¼ tsp. salt
½ tsp. nutmeg
1 tsp. cinnamon
1 tsp. vanilla

Cream sugar and shortening, add molasses and slightly beaten eggs. Beat thoroughly after adding vanilla.

Sift dry ingredients and add alternately with milk to the creamed mixture. Divide batter into 6 equal balls. This makes your 6 layers to stack. Put each ball in the center of a 9" cake pan. Press dough evenly to the edge of each pan, or you can roll out and cut into circles and bake on a cookie sheet. Either method, the pan should be greased. Bake at 350° for 10-12 minutes. Let cool slightly. Take a spatula to release edges. Tap pan lightly. Let cool and add hot filling between layers.

Dried Fruit Filling:

1 lb. dried apples
1 cup granulated sugar
½ cup brown sugar
½ tsp. nutmeg
½ tsp. cloves
1 tsp. cinnamon

Wash fruit, cover with water, cook until tender. You may pre-soak and cook in the water soaked in. If any water left in the cooked fruit, drain and reserve. Mash fruit enough to spread. If too thick to spread, add a little of the reserved juice. Spread hot mixture between layers.

If you are born lucky, even your roosters will lay eggs.
a Russian proverb

The desserts were a treat, because rarely did we have a dessert except on Sunday, or if we had company. They were made on Saturday, if they would keep until Sunday. We had no refrigeration in those days. Pound cake was very popular in the pioneer days, and we always had plenty of eggs, butter and milk. We had to be saving with sugar; it cost too much.

## AUNT LELA'S OLD TIMEY BUTTERMILK POUND CAKE
### circa 1914

1 cup butter (no substitute)
1 cup sugar (granulated)
1 cup brown sugar (packed)
4 eggs
¼ tsp. soda
1 cup buttermilk
3 cups flour
¼ tsp. salt
2 Tbsp. vanilla extract
2 Tbsp. lemon extract
1 tsp. almond extract

Cream butter and the sugar. Beat 2 eggs one at a time. Dissolve soda in buttermilk. Mix flour and salt and add to creamed mixture, alternately with buttermilk. Stir in flavorings. Pour in a 10" tube pan (well-greased and floured), and of course, there's PAM now. Bake in 350° oven for about 1 hour and 15 minutes. You can't believe the aroma from those extracts. I've used this recipe for many years.

Thanks to Margie Mize of McCalla, Alabama, for this wonderful recipe. You would die for a piece of this cake.

## CREAM CHEESE POUND CAKE
Margie Mize

3 cups sugar
3 sticks butter (real)
8 oz. cream cheese
6 eggs (brown eggs, richer)
3 cups flour (sifted 3 or 4 times)
1 Tbsp. vanilla (pure)
almond or lemon

Cream butter and cream cheese. Add sugar gradually, beat until fluffy. Add 1 egg at a time, beat well. Fold in flour gradually, beat until light. Add flavoring slowly. Pour into greased tube pan. To bake, start in 300° cold oven for 30 minutes, then 350° for 30 minutes or until done.

This cake stand has been in the family for nearly 100 years.
photograph by Michael Allen

I remember when Marie and I spent the summer with Aunt Sue she would make Yellow Buttermilk Cake. She made it because buttermilk was just about half the cost of sweet milk. I've had many requests for this cake, but had no luck finding it until I inherited Aunt Sue's recipe collection. There it was and labeled "Recipe For Yellow Buttermilk Cake." I was just about ready to create my own recipe.

## AUNT SUE'S
## YELLOW BUTTERMILK CAKE

4-5 eggs
3 cups sugar
3 cups flour
1 cup butter
1 tsp. vanilla
½ tsp. soda
1 cup buttermilk
¼ tsp. salt
juice of 2 lemons (sweetened, optional)

Cream butter and sugar. Add eggs one at a time. Beat well. Put soda with flour and sift. Add alternately with buttermilk. Add vanilla and beat well for a reasonable amount of time. Bake in moderate oven for about 1 hour. Rub on sweetened lemon juice.

**KITCHEN KAPERS:** When greasing pans, slip your hand in a sandwich bag It works perfectly for this purpose.

74

# CHERRY NUT CAKE
Gladys Moreau

1½ cup flour
1 Tbsp. baking powder
1 cup sugar
½ cup butter (less, if Oleo)
½ cup milk
¾ cup pie cherries (drained)
1 egg (beaten)
½ cup pecans (chopped)

Sift flour and baking soda together. Cream sugar and butter together, add flour, milk and egg gradually, mixing as you add. Stir in cherries and nuts. Bake in 9"x9" greased and floured pan at 325° for 30-45 minutes.

Sauce:
2 Tbsp. cornstarch
1 cup sugar
1½ cup cherry juice
½ cup butter
water

Sift together cornstarch and sugar. Mix the rest of the ingredients. Cook until clear and thick. Serve warm.

# GERMAN CHOCOLATE POUND CAKE

2 cups sugar
1 cup Crisco or butter
4 eggs
1 pkg. German sweet chocolate
1 cup buttermilk
2 tsp. vanilla flavoring
3 cups flour
½ tsp. salt
½ tsp. soda

Cream sugar and shortening until fluffy. Add 4 eggs, beat one at a time. Add flavoring with the buttermilk. Sift together flour, salt and soda. Add to the creamed mixture. Mix well. Add 1 package of chocolate that has been melted. Bake in a greased and floured 9" bunt pan at 300° for about 1½ hours. When done, leave in a tight fitting cake cover. Leave covered until cool. This is a good carry-out cake. Do not ice.

## FRESH APPLE CAKE

2 cups tart apples (chopped
        or grated)
1 cup sugar
½ cup salad oil
1 egg
½ cup flour (sifted)
½ tsp. cinnamon

¼ tsp. allspice
¼ tsp. nutmeg
¼ tsp. salt
1 tsp. soda
1 cup nuts

Pour sugar over apples. Let stand 20 minutes. Add egg and oil and stir well. Add flour, spices and nuts. Bake 30 - 40 minutes in oblong pan at 350°.

## CHOCOLATE PUDDING FILLING

This is a soft pudding and can be spread between layers and top of cake. A white icing may be put on top and let drizzle down sides.

2 squares unsweetened
    chocolate (grated)
1¼ cups milk
1 cup sugar
4 Tbsp. flour
2 Tbsp. butter
1 tsp. vanilla

Add grated chocolate to milk and melt over low heat. Beat until smooth with rotary beater. Sift flour and sugar together. Add small amount of chocolate milk to mixture and blend. Then beat with remainder of milk and beat until smooth and thickened. Add butter and vanilla. Beat until smooth. Cool and spread on cake,

This cake was such a treat during The Depression Days. After my mother died, my father, Aunt Maude and Uncle Jimmy bought joining lots and built a two-bedroom bungalow. Aunt Maude always cooked a special dinner on holidays, My father, Marie and I were always invited for Thanksgiving. I remember one particular Thanksgiving she had mincemeat cake. There was also baked hen and dressing. I never remembered Aunt Maude having recipes, like Aunt Sue did. They both were wonderful cooks and both taught us a lot about cooking. I remembered the cake being so good and often wished for the recipe. You can't imagine how glad I was to find this recipe, and now I'm sharing with you. It was in Aunt Sue's recipe collection that I inherited in the Spring of '97. I'm sure it could be a prize winner.

## AUNT MAUDE'S MINCEMEAT CAKE

1 cup applesauce
1 package of mincemeat
2 eggs
1 cup sugar
½ cup butter
1 cup nuts (chopped and fine)
1 tsp. vanilla
2 cups flour
1 tsp. baking powder
1 tsp. soda
½ tsp. salt
1 Tbsp. cocoa
½ tsp. cinnamon
½ tsp. allspice
　　　I leave the spices out. There's
　　　enough in the mincemeat
2 cups flour
1 cup hot water
or
½ cup, if homemade mincemeat
　　　is used

78

Cream butter and sugar and stir in beaten eggs. Add applesauce, nuts and vanilla. Add mincemeat which has been dissolved in the water. Sift dry ingredient together 3 times. Add to the mincemeat mixture. Bake in 4 layers and fill when cool.

## APRICOT FILLING FOR MINCEMEAT CAKE
or any cake

1 cup dried apricots
1½ cup brown sugar
1½ cups powdered sugar
1½ Tbsp. cornstarch
⅛ tsp. salt
2 Tbsp. lemon juice

Soak apricots in warm water for about 1 hour. Then bring to a boil and cook only 5 minutes. Put through food chopper. Drain pulp of excess juice, reserving 1 cup for the filling. Mix powdered sugar, cornstarch, salt; add apricot pulp. Cook in double boiler until thickens, stirring occasionally. Add lemon juice. Remove from heat. Beat until smooth. Let cool and spread between layers of cake. Good covered with 7 Minute Icing.

**KITCHEN KAPERS:** To soften brown sugar, put in tightly sealed plastic dish or a ziplock bag with a lettuce leaf, half of apple or slice of bread for about 12 hours. This will add moisture to the sugar. It works.

This recipe is so good and different. Good to serve when main course is scant. Good for "pot luck," if you want to show off your cooking skills. Prepare filling first.

## PINEAPPLE UPSIDE DOWN CAKE

Filling:

3 Tbsp. butter
1 cup coconut
½ cup dark brown sugar
        (packed)
⅓ cup cream
        or evaporated milk
¼ tsp. ginger (optional)
1 – #2 can of pineapple spears
        (drained)
9 maraschino cherries
        (optional)
10 blanched and peeled
        almonds

Melt the butter in bottom of 9" skillet. Sprinkle coconut around edge of pan, forming a circle. In center of pan pour the combined sugar, cream and ginger. Arrange the pineapple spears, nuts and cherries in a pattern in bottom of skillet over the mixture. Set aside.

Cake Batter:

3 eggs
1½ cup sugar
2 tsp. vanilla

¾ cup milk
1½ Tbsp. butter
1½ cups flour
1½ tsp. baking powder
½ tsp. salt

Beat eggs until thick and lemon colored. Gradually add sugar, beating well after each addition. Add vanilla. Add butter to hot milk. Sift dry ingredients and add to egg mixture, alternately with milk. Blend well. Pour over topping in pan. Bake at 350° for 40-50 minutes; cool 10 minutes before inverting on a serving plate.

Thanks to Elizabeth Tucker of Charlotte, Illinois, for this recipe. It's a favorite of her mother-in-law.

## EGGLESS, BUTTERLESS, MILKLESS CAKE
Elizabeth Tucker

Boil together for 3 minutes: 1 cup brown sugar, 1½ cup raisins, 1 cup water, ⅓ cup lard, pinch of salt. When cool, add 2 cups flour, 1 tsp. baking powder, 2 tsp. soda, 1 cup floured chopped nuts, 1 tsp. cinnamon, ½ tsp. cloves, ½ tsp. nutmeg, and 1 tsp. vanilla. Pour into a greased loaf pan and bake 40-45 minutes at 350°.

**KITCHEN KAPERS:** If cake sticks, hold pan over real low heat for 5-8 seconds. The cake will come out without splitting.

# UPSIDE DOWN
# CHOCOLATE CAKE
from Aunt Sue's collection

make topping first
Topping:
⅓ cup butter
1 cup light brown sugar
(packed) pecan halves

Melt the butter in the bottom of a heavy 10" skillet. Stir in sugar and set aside after placing the pecan halves in skillet.

cake batter:
1 cup butter
2 cups brown sugar
3 eggs
3 squares of unsweetened
        chocolate
2 cups flour (sifted)
½ cup of strong hot coffee
1 tsp. soda
1 tsp. baking powder
½ tsp. salt (I use less)
½ cup buttermilk
1 tsp. vanilla

Cream butter until soft. Gradually add the sugar and cream until light and fluffy. Add the eggs one at a time; beat well after each addition. Melt the chocolate in hot coffee. Stir into the sugar - butter mixture. Sift dry ingredients into flour, combine with the milk and vanilla. Spoon over the topping mixture in pan. Bake in 350° for 40-50 minutes. Remove to rack. Let set 3 minutes and release with spatula around the edges. Let cool another 3 minutes before turning upside down on serving plate. When cool, serve in wedges. This is a different cake and so delightfully delicious.

## TEXAS PECAN CAKE

Mrs. D.A. Smith
Segovia, Texas

1 cup melted butter
3 cups sugar
12 egg whites
1 cup milk
5 level cups flour (not sifted)
1 tsp. baking powder
1 quart pecans
2 tsp. lemon extract

Bake in the largest angel food cake pan. Put water under the rack. Cook in a slow oven 1 or 11/2 hours. Don't let brown 1st hour. This was written when everybody knew how to cook. This cake will freeze nicely. Why not divide into 2 cakes and freeze one.

Do good with what thou hast, or it will do thee no good,
William Penn

This recipe is from Aunt Sue's handwritten cookbook dated 1954. The recipe is by Sara Brashears, a friend of Aunt Sue's from Dimmitt, Texas.

## DEVIL'S FOOD SOUR CREAM CAKE

2 cups sugar
6 Tbsp. cocoa
2 tsp. soda
½ tsp. salt
1 tsp. vanilla
4 eggs
2 cups cake flour (sifted)
2 cups sour cream

Whip cream until thick and add sugar. Now add dry ingredients, alternate with beaten eggs. Grease and flour two 9" cake tins or bake in loaf pan. Bake in 325° oven for about 25-30 minutes. Use icing of your choice.

This recipe was handwritten by Aunt Sue in her 1927 P.T.A. cookbook.

## FUDGE UPSIDE DOWN CAKE

2 Tbsp. butter
¾ cup sugar
4 Tbsp. cocoa
2 tsp. baking powder
¼ tsp. salt
½ cup sweet milk
1 tsp. vanilla
½ cup nuts (chopped)

Melt butter and add sugar. Mix well. Add dry ingredients alternately with milk. Begin with flour and end with flour. Add vanilla and nuts. Pour into greased pan 1x8x12 inches. Do not flour or line pan.

Sauce:
½ cup white sugar
½ cup brown sugar
3 Tbsp. cocoa
1 square chocolate
1 cup sweet milk
1 Tbsp. butter
½ tsp. almond extract
½ cup nuts (chopped)

Heat ingredients for sauce. Stir until smooth. Pour over batter. This will be very thin. Bake at 350° about 35 minutes. The sauce will go to the bottom, making a rich, creamy topping. Serve with ice cream or whipped cream.

**KITCHEN KAPERS:** For greasing and flouring cake pans, try mixing together ½ cup Crisco, ½ cup vegetable oil and 1 cup flour and put on pans with a pastry brush. Keep in small covered plastic dish in refrigerator. Before using, put in microwave oven for a few seconds or let it get room temperature.

This recipe is a good way to use rancid mayonnaise if not too old. This cake was said to be used at the Waldorf Astoria Hotel in New York City.

## CHOCOLATE MAYONNAISE CAKE

2 cups flour (unsifted)
⅔ cup cocoa
¼ tsp. baking powder
1¼ baking soda (I use less)
1⅔ cup sugar
1 tsp. vanilla
1 cup mayonnaise
1⅓ cup water
3 eggs

In medium bowl mix together flour, cocoa, baking powder, soda. In larger bowl, beat eggs, vanilla and sugar at high speed until light and fluffy. Reduce to low speed and whip in mayonnaise. Add alternately with water and flour – adding and ending with flour. Bake in 2 layers and ice with favorite icing or bake in bunt pan without icing. Bake 350° until done.

## MY OLD STANDBY LOAF OR LAYER CAKE
Mrs. George Vierling, Sr.

Place 1½ cups sugar into mixing bowl, ½ cup butter, 3 whole eggs and 1 cup sweet milk. In a sifter put 2 cups silted flour, take out 6 Tbsp. flour and replace with 6 Tbsp. of cornstarch. Add 3 tsp. baking powder, pinch of salt and sift 3 times. Add flavoring; now add to the above ingredients. Sit down by the clock and beat from 5-7 minutes. (This was done by hand. If there were mixers then, nobody I knew had them.) The success of the cake depends on the beating. All measurements are to be leveled with a knife. Bake at 350° until done. About 40-50 minutes, less time if cooked in layers.

This recipe was handwritten in Aunt Sue's bank deposit book. This is the first cake I remember freezing.

## MOCK ANGEL FOOD CAKE
in memory of Aunt Sue

1 cup sugar
1 cup flour
1 cup sweet milk
pinch of salt
whites of 2 eggs
2 tsp. baking powder
½ tsp. vanilla
½ tsp. lemon extract
¼ tsp. almond extract


Sift sugar, flour, salt, and baking powder several times together. Bring milk to boil. Pour over dry mixture. Fold in vanilla, lemon and almond extract with slightly beaten egg whites last. Cook slowly 325° until golden brown.

# PUNCH BOWL CAKE

a modern recipe from
Sue Parker
Springfield, Tennessee

1 box yellow cake mix
2 cans of strawberry or cherry
    pie filling
1 large container of whipped
    topping
1 large can crushed pineapple
1 large box of vanilla instant
    pudding
1 cup nuts
½ cup maraschino cherries

Bake cake in 13x9x2 inch pan according to package directions. Cool. Cut into 2 inch squares. Mix pie filling as directed. Set aside. Using a large punch bowl begin layering 1 layer of cake square, top with cherry pie filling, whipped topping, pineapple, instant pudding, and nuts. Repeat layers. Top with whipped topping, nuts and cherries. Chill in refrigerator until ready to serve.

# TENNESSEE JAM CAKE

Sue Parker

1½ cups self-rising flour (sifted)
¼ tsp. soda
1½ tsp. cinnamon
1½ tsp. allspice
½ cup butter or margarine

½ cup sugar
3 whole eggs
½ cup buttermilk
½ cup blackberry jam
½ cup cherry preserves
¼ cup raisins (seedless)
½ cup pecans (finely
      chopped)

Heat oven to 350°. Grease thoroughly and lightly dust with flour two 8" round layer pans. Sift together flour, soda and spices. Cream together butter and sugar until light and fluffy. Beat in eggs one at a time. Fold in flour mixture and buttermilk, making 3 additions of each. Stir in preserves, raisins and nuts. Pour batter into prepared pans. Bake 30-35 minutes. Frost with carmel icing. This cake is better if allowed to mellow for 2-3 days.

## CARMEL ICING FOR JAM CAKE

2 cups sugar
½ cup buttermilk
1 stick butter
½ tsp. soda
½ tsp. vanilla
2 Tbsp. cocoa

Cook in saucepan. Beat until thickens and cool enough to spread on cake (top and sides).

# MISSISSIPPI MUD CAKE

2 sticks Oleo (margarine)
2 cups sugar
1½ cups flour
4 eggs
3 Tbsp. cocoa
1 Tbsp. vanilla
1⅓ cups coconut
1½ cups pecans (chopped)

Cream Oleo, sugar and cocoa. Add eggs and vanilla and mix. Add flour, coconut and nuts. Beat 2 minutes. Bake in 2 cake pans at 350° about 30 minutes. Spread with marshmallow cream and let cool completely.

Frost with:

1 box powdered sugar
1 stick Oleo (room temp.)
½ cup Milnot
⅓ cup cocoa
1 tsp. vanilla

Beat until smooth and spread between layers and frost sides and top.

# FRUIT COCKTAIL CAKE
Aunt Sue
circa 1954

1½ cup white sugar
2 cups flour
1½ tsp. soda
2 eggs
1 – #303 can fruit cocktail
or 1 heaping cup of fruit and
    ¾ cup juice
½ cup brown sugar
½ cup nuts (chopped)
    or coconut

Combine sugar, flour and soda. Add eggs and juice from cocktail. Mix until smooth. Fold in fruit and pour into oblong pan, greased and lined with wax paper. Roll finely chopped nuts into flour and mix with the brown sugar. Sprinkle over batter. The nuts will bake evenly through cake. Bake 325° for about 45 minutes. Leave in pan and pour the following topping over cake while still hot.

Topping:
½ cup white sugar
1 small can of milk
1 stick margarine

Boil these ingredients 5-8 minutes. Pour over cake.

A pessimist: When my ship comes in, I'll be at the airport.

These next 2 old recipes and the Lane Cake recipe were given to me by Nancy Widner Davis of Colquitt, Georgia. I met Nancy in Nashville, Tennessee, at the Country Christmas Craft Show at the Opryland Hotel where I have been an exhibitor for several years.

## JAPANESE FRUIT CAKE
### 75-100 year old recipe
We did not use this recipe during World War II.

2 sticks Oleo
2 cups sugar
4 eggs
3 cups flour (all purpose)
3 tsp. baking powder
1 cup milk
1 tsp. vanilla

Cream Oleo and sugar. Beat eggs one at a time. Sift flour and baking powder together and add alternately with milk to mixture. Add vanilla. Using half of the mixture, bake in layers at 400°. Mix the following together and add to remaining mixture. Bake in layers.

2 tsp. nutmeg
2 tsp. allspice
2 tsp. cinnamon
2 cups raisins

Icing or filling:
2 cups sugar
1 cup water
1 can coconut

1 large can pineapple
(crushed)
juice of 2 lemons

Mix ingredients together. Bring to a boil. Reduce heat to medium and boil for 15-20 minutes. Spread on cooled layers. Stack, alternating spice layers and plain layers. This is a favorite around Christmas and cold weather. This cake is very juicy and will mold quickly in hot weather.

This recipe is often referred to as "Poor Man's Fruitcake" and became famous back during The Depression during President Herbert Hoover's term in office.

## HOOVER CAKE

Boil 15 minutes and cool:
2 cups water
2 cups sugar
1 box raisins
almost ½ stick butter

Mix:
almost 2½ cups plain flour
2½ tsp. baking powder
vanilla flavoring
2 eggs
2 cups pecans

Combine sauce and batter. Bake in a tube pan in a 300° oven for about 1 hour and 15 minutes. Check with broom straw or a pick.

This recipe was given to me by Jeannette Weaver of Altus, Oklahoma. Her great-grandmother Sally Swayne Reden from Memphis, Tennessee, used this recipe. It has been used for 4-5 generations. It has to be old. I have had many calls for this recipe, and this is the only one I've found. When asked what it was like, nobody could tell me. They would only say, "I don't know; my grandmother and great-grandmother made it." Look for more of Jeannette Weaver's old family recipes in this cookbook. Jeannette hopes you enjoy these old Southern recipes as much as she and her family have.

## AMALGAMATION CAKE
amalgamation means
"the result of merger"

4 cups flour
4 egg whites (save yolks for
     later)
1 cup pecans (chopped)
1 cup raisins
1½ cup butter
1 cup buttermilk
2 cups sugar
2 tsp. cloves
2 tsp. cinnamon
2 tsp. cocoa
1 tsp. baking soda
1 pint blackberry jam

Mix and bake in 3 layers real slow in 300° oven.

Filling for cake:

1 cup sweet milk
4 egg yolks

2 cups sugar
1 cup butter

Cook until thick, then mix in:

2 cups pecans
2 boxes of raisins
2 cups fresh coconut (grated)

Spread filling between layers, on top and sides. This makes a very big cake, but remember everybody had large families. When there were family get-togethers, the cake was big enough to serve a lot of people. It's real rich, so serve in small pieces. Thank you, Jeannette, for this "long lost recipe."

**KITCHEN KAPERS:** If dried fruits and nuts are dredged in flour, they won't sink to the bottom. Use part of the flour called for in the recipe.

# LANE CAKE
Nancy Widner Davis

8 egg whites (beaten)
2 cups sugar
1½ cups butter
1 cup milk
4 cups flour
4 tsp. baking powder
1 tsp. vanilla

Cream butter and sugar. Add egg whites, milk, flour, baking powder, and vanilla. Bake layers at 425° until done.

Filling:
8 eggs yolks (beaten)
2 cups sugar
1 cup grape juice
1½ tsp. vanilla

Boil until the filling is thick.

Add:
1 cup coconut
1 cup raisins
1 lb. pecans (chopped)
1 tsp. vanilla

Stir well and spread between and on top of layers.

You can't achieve success without a purpose.

This recipe by Ruby Tisdale of Lebanon, Tennessee, was a favorite of her son, Wayne. He passed away in 1996 at the age of 38 of cancer. Wayne was a great singer, musician, artist, and cook. He was a friend and exhibitor at the craft shows where I exhibited. Wayne and his talents are missed.

## PRUNE CAKE
### in memory of Wayne Tisdale

2 cups sugar
2 cups flour
1 cup Wesson Oil
1 cup buttermilk
3 eggs
1 cup cooked prunes
    (chopped)
1 tsp. allspice
1 tsp. cinnamon
1 tsp. nutmeg
1 tsp. baking soda
1 tsp. vanilla
1 cup nuts (chopped)

Mix dry ingredients, add wet ingredients and mix well with mixer. Mixture will be thick. Bake at 350° for 45 minutes in a 13"x9"x2" (or larger) pan. When cooled, glaze:

Glaze:
½ cup butter
1 cup sugar
½ cup buttermilk
1 Tbsp. vanilla
1 tsp. soda
1 Tbsp. Karo syrup

Mix all but soda. Then add soda. Boil 2 minutes, Poke holes all over cake and pour glaze over top.

These next five recipes were given to me by my good friend, Wanda Briscoe of Altus, Oklahoma.

This cake was on Wanda Briscoe's grandmother's table every Christmas. It was layered real high on a cake stand. She always put a few nuts and maraschino cherries on top. This recipe is over 65 years old.

## CHINESE CHRISTMAS CAKE

1 cup butter
8 eggs
2 cups sugar
1 cup sweet milk
3 cups flour
1 cup pecans
1 box coconut
2 tsp. baking powder
2 tsp. vanilla
a pinch of cloves
1 tsp. cinnamon

Lemon Icing:

2 cups sugar
2 cups water (boiling)
juice of 2 lemons
juice of 2 oranges
1 box coconut
⅔ cups flour

Mix and boil until thick as honey (icing). There were no directions on how to mix the cake.

**KITCHEN KAPERS:** A good substitute for nuts: Brown 1 cup of quick cooking oatmeal in a little butter on low heat. Stir to keep from burning.

This is Wanda Briscoe's mother's recipe.

## MY MOTHER'S CAKE
in memory of Vira Jane Ford

Cream:
2 cups sugar
1 cup shortening

Add:
4 eggs (beaten well)
3 cups flour
¼ tsp. soda
½ tsp. salt
1 tsp. lemon flavoring
1 tsp. orange flavoring

Cook in angel food cake pan at 350°
until done.

Pour over cake while still warm:

Boil:
1 cup sugar
1 cup orange juice

"It is God that girdeth me with strength,
and maketh my way perfect."
Psalm 18:32

# MINCEMEAT PIE
Wanda Briscoe

1 cup sugar
2 Tbsp. flour
½ tsp. salt
¾ cup butter (melted)
3 eggs
¾ cups pecans (chopped)
1 cup (Nonesuch) mincemeat
     in the jar

Combine sugar, flour and salt. Mix in butter. Beat in eggs one at a time. Pour into 9" pie shell and bake at 375° for 35 minutes.

# BLUEBERRY PIE
Wanda Briscoe

1 – 10 oz. can blueberries
2½ Tbsp. cornstarch
¾ cups sugar
1 tsp. lemon juice

Cook until thick and let cool.

2 bananas

Slice bananas and line graham cracker crust, then pour blueberry mixture over bananas. To whipped cream, add powdered sugar (about ¼ cup), 1 tsp. vanilla and 1 tsp. gelatine. Let set up in refrigerator.

This recipe is for ½ gallon ice cream (parlor) maker. You use table salt and ice cubes to freeze it. All of Wanda Briscoe's grandchildren love this ice cream. It can be put in the freezer and makes really good ice cream cones.

## STRAWBERRY BANANA ICE CREAM
Wanda Briscoe

1 can condensed milk (Eagle brand)
1 box frozen strawberries (sweet)
2 large bananas (mashed with fork)
2½ pints whipped cream
1½ pint half and half

Boil ½ cup water and ½ box strawberry Jell-O (let cool). Mix and freeze.

## SWEETENED CONDENSED MILK
you can make your own
for economy and convenience

1 cup powdered skim milk,
⅓ cup water,
⅔ cup granulated sugar
¼ cup butter or Oleo.

Measure in blender. Blend until smooth. Use as you would any sweetened condensed milk.

# OLD TIMEY CHESS PIE

½ cup butter (melted)
2 cups sugar
1 Tbsp. corn meal
1 Tbsp. vinegar
4 eggs (lightly beaten)
1 tsp. vanilla

Combine sugar and meal. Add remaining ingredients in order given. Beat well. Place in a 9" unbaked pie shell. Bake 350° oven for 15 minutes then reduce to 300° and bake 30-40 minutes until golden brown or until knife inserted comes out clean.

In the pioneer days, lemons were sometimes scarce. If you had one, you could make this lemon chess pie; otherwise, you would make the Old Timey Chess Pie.

# LEMON CHESS PIE

2 cups sugar
2 Tbsp. meal
1 Tbsp. flour
4 eggs (slightly beaten)
¼ cup lemon juice
½ tsp. vanilla
3 Tbsp. lemon peel (grated)

Blend sugar, meal and flour. Stir eggs in sugar mixture. Add the rest of ingredients. Bake in 350° oven 30-40 minutes until light brown.

# FRIED PIES

Sweet dried fruit was used for this fried pie. Use Rich Biscuit Dough on page 120. Roll in 4-6 inch circles. Fill half of this circle with 1 heaping Tbsp. of sweetened dried fruit. Moisten edges with water, fold over to form a semi-circle and press edges together with a fork. Fry in hot skillet in about 2" of hot grease or less. More may have to be added. Turn only once while frying. Now, we would drain on paper towels.

## EASY APPLE DUMPLINGS
(Mexican)
Patsy Hunt
Nashville, TN

Melt about ¼ cup Oleo in bottom of 9x13 inch pan. Peel and chop 3 or 4 apples. Sprinkle with sugar and cinnamon. Dot with Oleo. Place ½ cup of apples in tortilla and roll. Place with the seam down in melted Oleo. Dissolve ½-¾ cup of sugar in enough water (about 2 cups) to barely cover apples. Pour over tortilla, bake covered 30 minutes at 350°. Uncover and bake another 30 minutes. Patsy vows you would die for them.

How do you know love is gone? If you said you'd be there by seven, and you got there by nine, and he or she hadn't called the police or hospital – it's gone.

Marlene Dietrich

# PRIZE WINNING PEACHY PIE
modern

Crust:
⅔ cups Crisco
2 cups flour
1 tsp. salt
2 Tbsp. butter
6-7 Tbsp. peach syrup

Cut shortening into flour and salt until size of peas. Sprinkle peach syrup over flour mixture, stir until dough holds together. Roll out half of ball on a floured dough board to ⅛" thickness. Fit into a 9" pie plate. Set aside until ready to assemble. Roll out remaining dough, cut into about 6-7 circles. Brush with peach syrup. This is to decorate the top. Cut a collar of foil to cover the edge of pie. Measure the circle by the pie plate. Cut and then cut another circle 1½ - 2" smaller. When you have pie assembled, this prevents the crust from getting too brown.

Peaches in cheesecake filling:
1 lb. and 13 oz. of canned sliced peaches (cling)
½ cup and ⅓ cup sugar
2 Tbsp. cornstarch
2 Tbsp. corn syrup
2 tsp. of pumpkin pie spice
1 tsp. vanilla

Drain peaches and reserve juice. Combine peach slices, ⅓ cup sugar, cornstarch and corn syrup, pumpkin pie spices, and vanilla. This is your filling. Leave in pan until ready to assemble.

Cheesecake topping:
2 eggs (slightly beaten)
⅓ cup sugar
1 Tbsp. lemon juice
1 pkg. (3 oz.) of cream cheese
        at room temperature
½ cup dairy sour cream
2 Tbsp. peach syrup

Combine eggs, ⅓ cup sugar, lemon juice, 2 Tbsp. peach syrup in small saucepan. Cook stirring constantly until thick. Blend sour cream with softened cheese. Add hot mixture. Beat smooth. Now you are ready to assemble the pie.

Pour the peach filling in the 9" crust, Dot with 2 Tbsp. of butter. Now pour the topping over the filling and decorate with the circles that go on last. Bake at 425° for 10 minutes, reduce to 350° and cook 30-40 minutes until a deep golden brown. Now, it's time to call me. Good for when "company's a coming."

I've had so many calls for this recipe. Now, I know why. they are so good! There's no telling how old this recipe is. Aunt Lela was born around 1890.

## AUNT LELA'S VINEGAR ROLLED DUMPLINGS

I make the dumplings first.
2 cups flour
¼ tsp. salt
1 tsp. sugar
3 tsp. baking powder
2 Tbsp. lard
or 2 Tbsp. Crisco (heaping)

Mix salt, sugar and baking powder in flour. Cut in shortening in the flour as you would for a pie crust. Stir in 4-6 Tbsp. of water – enough to handle well. When enough water, the dough will follow the spoon around the bowl. Roll very thin like pie crust. Cut into strips about 1½" wide, then into squares. Set aside until the vinegar mixture is ready.

Vinegar mixture:
5 cups water
1 cup sugar
¼ tsp. salt
1 Tbsp. butter (heaping)
1 cup apple cider vinegar

Mix the first 4 ingredients and bring to a rolling boil. Now add the cup of apple cider vinegar. Let come to a rolling boil again and add dumplings one at a time and never let it cease to boil. Cover. When done the dumplings will be transparent and will be fairly tender. It will take about 30 minutes. For variation, add 1-2 pints of fresh or canned blackberries, sweetened to taste, to the vinegar pie. This will give you a sweet sour blackberry cobbler. Try it, you'll like it. I'll guarantee it!

This recipe was given to me by Pearl's granddaughter, Helen Sloan Peyton. Pearl live to be 104 years old (1886-1990). She moved to Jackson County, Oklahoma, from Texas at an early age and lived there most all of her 104 years. This recipe has been used for at least four generations and probably more. It is written verbatim. The old recipes had very little instructions.

## PEARL SLOAN'S BIG CUSTARD PIE

3 eggs
2 cups of rich milk
or use some butter
½ cup sugar plus 1 Tbsp. sugar

Don't beat eggs too long. We brown butter. Pour in crust or bake without crust.

**KITCHEN KAPERS:** Brush top of 2 crust pies with milk, evaporated is better. It will brown better and will eliminate drying when freezing.

# VINEGAR ROLLS
an old recipe that was used often,
but long forgotten
circa 1880

Combine 2 cups of sugar and ¾ cup of apple cider vinegar, bring to a boil and let simmer while preparing the dough.

Mixing of dough:

In large mixing bowl, put 3½ cups flour, 3 tsp. baking powder, ⅛ tsp. salt. Cut in 1 cup shortening. Now make a deep well in center of mixture and pour in 2 cups of milk. Mix into a stiff dough. Put a little flour on dough board and roll very thin. Spread soft butter (2 or 3 sticks) over dough – just sliver it on. Sprinkle well with sugar and cinnamon mixture – about ½ cup of sugar and 4 tsp. cinnamon. Roll up and cut in slices. Seal the edges with water. Place in a 9½"x11" pan with cut side down. When rolling out dough, start with long side and seal edge with water. Pour the boiling hot mixture over rolls. Bake 350° oven about 30 minutes or until golden brown.

Mrs. White was noted for her baked custard. She took a lot of it to the sick. She made the best in "the whole wide world." It was made in a casserole. The secret she said was to cook in a real slow oven and never let it boil. If she used custard cups, they were put in a large skillet of hot water.. If she used a casserole, she would put the casserole in a large pan of hot water ½" from the top of the custard. She said the hot water kept the custard from having a tough skim on top. I've always heard, if you could make a perfect baked custard, you could cook anything. That was certainly true of Minnie White.

## MINNIE WHITE'S BAKED CUSTARD

3 cups milk (scalded)
4 eggs (slightly beaten)
¼ tsp. salt
½ cup sugar (no more or
       no less)
1 tsp. vanilla.

Scald milk carefully. It's scalded when it begins to bubble around edges. Beat the eggs lightly, blend with sugar and salt. Pour egg mixture into the milk and stir constantly. Add the vanilla. At this point, strain to remove the egg anchors. She never did, and it was still delicious. You can sprinkle nutmeg over the top if you choose. Bake in slow oven 325° until knife inserted in center comes out clean – 40-50 minutes for cups or 60 minutes for casserole.

# PECAN PIE
in memory of Floyd Robinson

¼ cup butter or margarine
½ cup sugar
1 cup dark corn syrup
¼ tsp. salt
3 eggs
1½ cup pecans (chopped)

Cream butter and sugar until fluffy. Add corn syrup and salt. Beat well. Add eggs one at a time, beating well after each addition. Stir in pecans. pour into 9" unbaked pastry shell. Bake at 350° for 45-50 minutes or until knife comes out clean.

This recipe was given to me at least 30 years ago by Mrs. W. W. Williams.

# OATMEAL PIE

1 pie shell (unbaked)
3 eggs (slightly beaten)
½ cup Oleo (margarine)
1 cup dark corn syrup
½ cup sugar
1 tsp. vanilla
⅛ tsp. salt
1½ cups oatmeal

Combine eggs and Oleo in bowl. Stir in the rest of the ingredients and mix well. Pour into shell. Bake in 350° oven for 50 minutes. It resembles a pecan pie only not as rich.

# BUTTERMILK PIE
Jeannette Weaver

2 cups buttermilk
2 cups sugar
5 large egg yolks (reserve
    whites)
2 heaping Tbsp. cornstarch
2 tsp. vanilla
1 Tbsp. butter (melted)

Mix together sugar, cornstarch and buttermilk. Stir in beaten egg yolks and melted butter. Cook in pan on top of stove, stirring constantly until thick. Pour into baked pie shell. Use egg whites for meringue. Put meringue on top of pie and bake in 400° oven until golden brown.

# AUNT MAUDE'S RHUBARB PIE

Place in bottom of unbaked pie shell 2-2½ cups of slices of rhubarb, frozen or fresh. Sprinkle 2 Tbsp. of lemon juice over rhubarb. Beat 3 eggs real well, gradually beat in scant 1 cup of sugar. Add a pinch of salt. Stir in 2 Tbsp. melted butter to the custard. Pour mixture over rhubarb. Start at 400° oven for 10 minutes, reduce heat to 325° and bake for about 30 minutes until custard is set. You've missed a lot, if you haven't made this pie.

Keep you face to the light, and the shadows will fall behind you.

# MARIE MILLS'
# PERFECT MERINGUE

Beat 3 egg whites (room temperature). When they begin to foam, add ¼ tsp. cream of tartar. Now beat in ⅔ cup sugar. Sprinkle in slowly and beat well after each addition. Beat until you can not feel any sugar crystals between your fingers. When this is beaten so it stands in small peaks, fold in remaining sugar and ½ tsp. vanilla. Use mixing spoon and fold in as carefully as you would an Angel Food Cake. Pile the meringue over the thoroughly cooled pie. Bake in a 350° oven. It will start to brown in 8 minutes. It will be done in 10-12 minutes. When done, place on wire rack free from draft to cool.

Never skimp on meringue. For an attractive appearance, place in rough mounds. To cut pie, cut through the meringue only, then clean knife and cut through filling and crust.

## FOR PERFECT PIE CRUST
see Glazed Apple Pie
on page 116

**KITCHEN KAPERS:** Buttermilk can be substituted for sour cream in most recipes. Try it sometime.

## WEEPLESS MERINGUE
Lois Phillips
New Boston, Missouri

Moisten 1 Tbsp. cornstarch with 2 tsp. water. Stir above mixture in ½ cup boiling water. Cook over low heat until thickened, stirring constantly. Set aside to cool. Make regular meringue, gradually beat in cooled cornstarch and beat until it forms stiff peaks, but not too dry. Put on pie, sealing edges.

## BARBARA'S CHEESE WAFERS
Barbara Stovall
Iva, SC

1 cup grated sharp cheese
1 stick butter
1 cup plain flour
½ cup pecans (chopped)
¼ tsp. ground red pepper

Preheat oven to 375°. Mix well. Make small long rolls. (quarter size). Chill overnight. Slice thin. Place on pan that has been sprayed with PAM. Bake 12-14 minutes.

Mrs. Mills was born in 1863. She was my sister's mother-in-law.

## MRS. MILLS'
## PUMPKIN CUSTARD PIE

1½ cups sweet milk
½ cup cream
  or small can evaporated
  milk works well
4 eggs
½ cup white sugar
½ cup brown sugar (packed)
3 Tbsp. flour
¼ tsp. salt
1 tsp. cinnamon
½ tsp. ginger
½ tsp. allspice
1 tsp. vanilla or lemon extract
  (I use both)

Mix flour, sugar, salt, and spices together. Mix the eggs with the milk. Now stir in the flour and sugar mixture. Add vanilla and/or lemon extract. Before putting in crust, run the whites of an egg over bottom of crust. This prevents the crust from getting soggy. Bake for 10 minutes at 425° and reduce heat to 300°. Bake 45-60 minutes until knife inverted in center comes out clean.

A time for everything, a time to be born, a time to die, a time to plant and a time to harvest.

Ecclesiastes 3:1-2

You'll have to hide this pie for it to keep.

## AUNT SUE'S
## SOUR CREAM APPLE PIE

1 cup tart apples (chopped)
¾ cup sugar
2 Tbsp. flour
1½ cups of sour cream
1 egg (well beaten)
¼ tsp. salt
1 tsp. vanilla

Mix sugar and flour, then add cream, egg, vanilla, and salt. Beat until smooth. Add apples and mix thoroughly. Pour in unbaked pie shell. Bake in 450° oven for 15 minutes. Reduce heat to 325° and bake for 30 minutes. Now you add a topping; a real neat trick to know.

Topping:
½ cup brown sugar
1 tsp. cinnamon
½ cup flour
½ cup butter

Mix thoroughly and sprinkle over pie. Return to oven and bake another 30 minutes or less at 350°.

**KITCHEN KAPERS:** Why not put in 1 cup of cottage cheese and 2 tsp. lemon juice in blender, blend until real creamy, and you have a good substitute for sour cream.

This was a favorite recipe of Fern Tims. It's a Crisco recipe; there is no date, and the paper she had copied it on is real old. According to Fern, nobody made shortening but Crisco. Fern always said, "Try this apple pie for something that's different, delicious, tasty, and attractive."

## GLAZED APPLE PIE
in memory of Fern Tims

6 cups of apple slices (about 6
    medium size tart apples)
½ cup seedless raisins
    (optional)
¾ cup sugar
1 tsp. cinnamon
⅛ tsp. salt
2 Tbsp. orange juice
3 Tbsp. butter

Toss apples and raisins with the combined sugar, flour, cinnamon, and salt. Turn in a 9" pastry lined pie plate. Sprinkle with orange juice and dot with butter. Cover with top crust and seal and flute edges. Slit top crust near center for steam escape. Bake for 10 minutes at 450° and then reduce to 350° until desired brownness, and apples are tender. Add melted butter last and spread orange glaze ove hot pie. Mix glaze in order given.

Orange Glaze:

1 cup powdered sugar
    (sift, if lumpy)

1 tsp. orange peel (grated)
2 Tbsp. orange juice

Spread orange glaze over hot pie.

Fern would never forgive me if I didn't give you this Crisco crust recipe. It is the most detailed and plainest instructions one could have.

## PIE CRUST FOR
## TWO CRUST 9" PIE

2 cups flour (sifted)
1 tsp. salt
¾ cup Crisco
¼ cup water

Pre-heat oven. Sift flour before measuring. Spoon lightly into measuring cup and level without shaking or packing. Combine salt and flour in a mixing bowl. With a pastry blender cut Crisco until uniform. Sprinkle with water a little at a time. Mix with a fork. Work dough into a small ball with hands. Divide dough into 2 parts and press into small circles with smoothness on a lightly floured dough board. Roll bottom crust about 1½ " circle larger than the top crust. Measure, by the inverted pie plate. Turn edge even with plate. Add filling. Roll top crust the same way. Seal the 2 crusts and flute.

When Marie's grandsons, Robb and Matthew Mills, earn honors at school, and there are lots of them, she rewards them with their favorite food. It might be banana pudding, chocolate pie, chicken fried steak or chicken and dumplings. Their favorite, I suppose, is the Pineapple Pie. It's their daddy's favorite, too.

## MARIE MILLS'
## TWO CRUST PINEAPPLE PIE

1 large can pineapple
(crushed and
unsweetened)
1 cup sugar
2 Tbsp. water
¼ cup cornstarch
2 Tbsp. butter

Blend cornstarch with sugar. Rinse the can out with about 2 Tbsp. of water. Put in heavy saucepan with the butter and cook until it begins to thicken. Let cook slightly. Put in unbaked pie shell. Cut a circle for the top crust about 1½", smaller than the bottom. This eliminates flutting, and you don't slit for air vents. Brush top with sweet milk; evaporated milk is better. Sprinkle with sugar. Start in 400° oven for 10 minutes, then reduce heat to 350° and bake until golden brown.

**KITCHEN KAPERS:** If a recipe calls for thin cream, use ⅞ cup milk with 3 tsp.. of vegetable oil (for 1 cup).

# Cobbler and Canning

We called them cobblers, but they were more like dumplings. The dough was made from the Rich Biscuit Dough recipe on page 120, cut into strips and then into squares like chicken dumplings. They were then dropped in the boiling fruit with the juice.

Cobblers were made when company was coming. Many times there would be 10 or more at the table. The kids would have to wait to eat. We were too busy playing to object. There were five in our family, and most families had more. For that reason the fruit was canned in half gallon jars.

Any kind of fruit could be used, canned or fresh. We used lots of dried fruit, because it called for no refrigeration. We canned wild green grapes gathered from the creek bottom before the seeds matured. Wild plum thickets were on the roadside, in the pasture or just about everywhere. The sand plums were said to be brought here by the Indians. Wild plums made the best jelly, and now you can find it on the grocery shelf – a pretty good substitution. Peaches were canned when the freeze didn't get them. The fruit was canned by cooking until done, put into sterilized jars and sealed. Tomatoes were canned the same way. Most vegetables were canned by the Hot Bath System. Pickles and relishes were preserved with vinegar and sealed while hot. Cucumber pickles were used for potato salad. There were also peach pickles and beet pickles. Peach pickles were so good with that country ham, and we saved the juice to glaze the ham.

The canned goods, as we called them, were stored in a hand-dugged cellar, often called a dugout or storm cellar. It was very crude. The floors, wall, and even the shelves were dirt. The only things it took to build a cellar were wood for the ceiling, wood for door frame, the door and lots of hard labor. The top was covered with lots of dirt.

# FRUIT COBBLERS

Make the dough first from the recipe, Rich Biscuit Dough. Roll thin like pie crust, Cut in strips, then into small squares. Let set while preparing the fruit. Sweeten ½ gallon fruit to taste. Add more water if you want more juice. Let fruit come to rolling boil. Add about 2 Tbsp. butter. Never let the juices stop boiling. Add the dumplings in boiling fruit one at a time. Boil until tender and the dumplings are transparent for 15-20 minutes. The dumplings made with baking powder will thicken the juice. Any fresh fruit could be used. Nothing is any better than the fresh peaches or blackberries in cobblers.

## RICH BISCUIT DOUGH
to be used for fruit cobblers, fruit dumplings
or fried pies
circa 1885

2 cups flour
½ tsp. salt
2 Tbsp. sugar
4 Tbsp. baking soda
4 Tbsp. shortening
¾ cup sweet milk

Sift dry ingredients and cut in short-ening. Add milk to make a dough that's easily handled. Turn out on a floured board and roll like you would a pie crust (very thin about ⅛").

I'm only giving you a few recipes for cream pies. You can find them in most cookbooks, or you may already have your favorite one. Why not uses the basic cream pie? There are so many variations: banana, coconut, chocolate, pineapple, carmel (with brown sugar, instead of white), date, or anything you can dream up. Be a creative cook! They all have 2 things in common; they are put in a baked crust and covered with a meringue or whipped topping. Good luck! But you won't need it after you master a few easy cooking techniques.

## BASIC CREAM PIE

¾ cup sugar
4 Tbsp. flour
a pinch of salt
3 egg yolks (well beaten)
egg whites for meringue
2 cups milk
1 tsp. vanilla 2 Tbsp. butter

Blend sugar, flour and salt; add gradually to the eggs. Add milk to the sugar/egg mixture and put in heavy saucepan on medium heat and beat constantly until thickens. Add butter and vanilla last. Put in baked pie shell and add meringue and bake. See page 112 for Marie Mills' Perfect Meringue recipe.

"He that is slow to anger is better than the mighty;
and he that ruleth his spirith than he that taketh a city."
Proverbs 16:32

# CHOCOLATE CREAM PIE
everybody's favorite

3 squares of chocolate
2½ cups cold sweet milk
4 Tbsp. flour
1 cup sugar
¼ tsp. salt 4 egg yolks
      (beaten slightly)
2 Tbsp. butter
2 tsp. vanilla

Scald the milk with the chocolate. Beat until smooth. Mix together flour, sugar and salt. Add to egg yolks. Beat well. Pour the chocolate mixture over egg yolks a little at a time. Put in a double boiler or finish cooking in a heavy saucepan, cook until thicken. You'll need to stir constantly. Pour in a baked pie shell and cover with meringue.

# APPLE BROWN BETTY
Aunt Sue

4 cups tart apples
      (chopped fine)
1 cup sugar
½ cup water
1 tsp. nutmeg
a dash of salt

Place in bottom of baking dish.

Mix:

1 cup flour
½ cup brown sugar
½ cup butter

Sprinkle over first mixture. Bake 45-50 minutes in a 350° oven.

This has to be an old Southern recipe. The first time I heard of this recipe, a serviceman returning from Vietnam requested a Sugar Pie that his grandmother had made. His mother was searching diligently for this recipe. I hope she found it.

## SUGAR PIE

3 eggs (beaten)
5 Tbsp. sugar
3 Tbsp. flour
a pinch of salt dash of nutmeg
        or cinnamon
2 cups milk
2 Tbsp. butter (melted)

Mix flour and sugar together. Add eggs gradually to the flour mixture. Add cinnamon and milk, beat. With 2 Tbsp. melted butter, put in 9" pie shell. Then place on a cookie sheet to bake. Bake at 350° for 35-40 minutes.

Spinning a rope is lots of fun – providing your neck ain't in it.
        Will Rogers

This is an old Pennsylvania dish well know to old Dutch families.

## SHOOFLY PIE

½ cup brown sugar
10 Tbsp. molasses
1 egg (slightly beaten)
½ cup butter (melted)
½ cup of strong hot coffee
½ tsp. soda
¾ cup flour
½ tsp. salt
½ tsp. cinnamon
½ tsp. clove

Mix well and pour in 9" unbaked pie shell. Alternate filling and crumb mixture. Start with crumb mixture on bottom.

Crumb mixture:
⅔ cup flour
½ cup brown sugar
¼ cup butter

Line a deep 9' pie pan with crust. Dot with crumb section first then alternate with filling with crumb mixture. Bake in hot oven 400° for 15 minutes, then 350° until filling is set for about 40 minutes.

**KITCHEN KAPERS:** To keep fruit from turning dark, place peeled in a bowl of cool water with 2 crushed vitamin C tablets.

124

This is my son's favorite pie. He says, " I'll guarantee you can't stop at just 1 piece."

# TWO CRUST CHERRY PIE

2 – 16 oz. of tart cherries with
      juice
¾ cup sugar
¼ cup cornstarch and 1 Tbsp.
      cornstarch
1 tsp. cinnamon
½ cup sugar
1 Tbsp. butter (no substitute)
½ tsp. almond extract
5 drops of red food coloring
> If my food color had dried up, it
> didn't bother my son. He said it
> tasted just as good.

Drain cherries, reserving 1 cup juice, set cherries aside. Combine ¾ cup sugar, cornstarch and cinnamon in medium saucepan. Stir to remove lumps. Stir cherry juice into sugar mixture. Cook over medium heat. Stir ring constantly until smooth and thickened. Remove from heat and carefully stir in cherries, margarine ½ cup sugar, extract, and food coloring, if desired. Keep cherries whole. Follow Marie Mills' Two Crust Pineapple Pie on page 118 for crust recipe. Bake at 425° for 10 minutes, then 350° until brown.

# CHOCOLATE BOURBON PECAN PIE
Ray Moreau

¾ cup sugar
¼ cup cornstarch
3 eggs
½ cup light syrup
½ cup margarine (melted)
¼ cup bourbon
1 cup pecan (coarsely
    chopped)
6 oz. semi-sweet chocolate
    pieces
1 pie shell (unbaked)

In a large bowl with mixer on low speed, stir together sugar and cornstarch. Beat in eggs until well blended. With mixer at medium speed, beat in corn syrup, margarine and bourbon until well blended. With wooden spoon, stir in pecans and chocolate pieces. Pour into pastry shell. Bake in 350° oven for 50-60 minutes or until set around edges. Cool on wire rack.

**KITCHEN KAPERS:** For pies that don't have a meringue, pre-cook crust 5-7 minutes at 375° before filling. This will prevent curst from being undercooked.

126

# DATE PIE
Bobbie Woodard
a great modern dessert


2 cups sugar
1 Tbsp. (heaping) flour
1 cup milk
4 eggs (beaten)
1 cup Oleo or butter
1 cup dates (cut into 3 pieces)
1 cup  nuts (chopped)

Mix and cook over low heat, stirring constantly until thick. Cool and pour into a baked pie shell. Makes 2 pies. Top with whipped cream.

# BANANA PIE
Bobbie Woodard
another one of Bobbie's delicious pies


8 oz. cream cheese (room temperature)
1 can condensed milk (Eagle brand)
½ cup lemon juice
1 cup whipped cream
2 bananas
1 baked pie shell

Slice bananas in bottom of shell. Mix the other 4 ingredients. Fold in whipped cream last. Refrigerate.


Politics has got so expensive that it takes lots of money even to get beat with.
Will Rogers

Jeff Davis Pie was first made by Aunt Jule Ann, a slave in the family of George B. Warren of Dover, Missouri. Before the Civil War, the Warren family moved from the South to Missouri, taking his slaves with him, including Aunt Jule Ann, who was the queen of the Warren kitchen. One Sunday with distinguished guests at the dinner table, Aunt Jule Ann served a new kind of pie that was so delicious that everyone wanted to know how it was made. Aunt Jule Ann, who was an admirer of Jefferson Davis, declared, "That's Jeff Davis Pie."

## JEFF DAVIS PIE

3 eggs (separated)
1 cup sugar
2 cups sweet milk
½ cup butter
5 Tbsp. flour
1 tsp. cinnamon
½ tsp. nutmeg
½ tsp. allspice
½ tsp. cloves

Mix dry ingredients. Add milk and beat until smooth. Cook in a heavy pan over low heat until thickens. Add butter while cooking. Add very slowly, the beaten eggs, beating constantly and continue beating until smooth. Cover with meringue.

I have been a fan of Abraham Lincoln ever since I can remember. He was reared under the direst of circumstances. He remained very poor until he became a lawyer (self-taught) and licensed in 1837. It wasn't until then did things gradually began to look up. He had only one year of "schooling," but he had such a burning desire to learn. Lincoln would lie in front of the fire at night, the fire being his only light, and do sums with a piece of wood for a slate. Unlike the typical frontiersman, he never made a hunter or pulled a trigger on anything larger than a wild turkey. To me Lincoln was the most outstanding man of the 19th century and for all the centuries to come. Edgar Allan Poe is said to be the greatest genius of poetry, and I would say that Lincoln is the genius of prose. So it's no wonder that I would want this beautiful piece of literature in my book.

### The Gettysburg Address

"Fourscore and seven years ago our fathers brought forth on this continent a new nation conceived in liberty and dedicated to the proposition that all men are created equal. Now we are engaged in a great civil war testing whether that nation, or any nation so conceived and so dedicated, can long endure. We are met on a great battlefield of that war. We have come to dedicate a portion of that field as a final resting-place for those who here gave their lives that that nation might live. It is altogether fitting and proper that we should do this. But, in a larger sense, we cannot dedicate, we cannot consecrate, we cannot hallow this ground. The brave men, living and dead, who struggled here have consecrated it far above our poor power to add or detract. The world will little note nor long remember what we say here, but it can never forget what they did here. It is for us the living rather to be dedicated here to the unfinished work which they who fought here have thus far so nobly advanced. It is rather for us to be here dedicated to the great task remaining before us – that from these honoured dead we take increased devotion to that cause for which they gave the last full measure of devotion – that we here highly resolve that these dead shall not have died in vain, that this nation under God shall have a new birth of freedom, and that government of the people, by the people, for the people, shall not perish from the earth."

The main address on that occasion was 2 hours in length by Edward Everett, the best known orator of the time, and received unqualified praise. No one paid attention to Lincoln's address. It is interesting, however, to know that Edward Everett wrote to Mr. Lincoln on the day following the address, saying: "I wish that I could flatter myself that I had come as near to the central idea of the occasion in 2 hours as you did in 2 minutes."

Betty McMillan has used this recipe over 50 years.

# SUET PUDDING
Betty McMillan
Marion, IL

1¾ cup all purpose flour
(sifted)
1 tsp. salt
1 tsp. soda
1 tsp. cinnamon
¼ tsp. ginger
¼ tsp. cloves
¼ tsp. nutmeg
¾ cup molasses
¾ cup suet (ground)
¾ cup milk
2 qts. water (in pressure cooker
with rack)

Sift flour with all dry ingredients. Mix molasses, sweet milk and suet. Combine liquid and dry ingredients and mix well. Pour into a buttered 1 quart mold. Cover with wax paper, tie securely. Place on rack with water in cooker. Steam 20 minutes with petcock open. Close petcock and cook 50 minutes at 10 lbs. pressure.

Life is so uncertain, why don't we eat the dessert first?

Elizabeth Tucker gave me this recipe which is a favorite of her father. He thought I should have in my cookbook. Thanks to both of you.

## PERSIMMON PUDDING
Elizabeth Tucker
Charleston, IL

2 cups persimmon pulp
1 egg
½ cup sugar
¼ cup margarine (melted)
2 cups flour
2 cups milk
½ tsp. nutmeg
½ tsp. cinnamon
½ tsp. soda
½ tsp. vanilla

Beat eggs slightly and beat in sugar, melted margarine and vanilla. Sift dry ingredients together and add alternately with milk. Pour in a greased 9x13x2 inch pan. Bake 2 hours at 250°

This crock has been in my home as long as I can remember.
photograph by Michael Allen

# SWEET POTATO PUDDING
## Tennessee Style

½ lb. butter (melted)
2 cups sugar (1 cup brown - 1
    cup white)
4 cups raw sweet potatoes
    (grated)
4 eggs (slightly beaten)
1 tsp. cinnamon
½ tsp. nutmeg
½ tsp. cloves
½ tsp. salt
2 cups sweet milk

Mix sugars in melted butter, add eggs gradually. Stir in spices and salt. Add milk and grated potatoes. Mix well. Nuts or coconut could be added. In the past there were just the spices to flavor the sweet potato. Serve with butter sauce.

Butter sauce:

¼ cup butter
1 tbsp. brandy flavoring
1 cup powdered sugar

Mix. Add alternately the brandy flavoring. Put 1 tsp. on top of each serving, when ready to serve.

To ease another's heartache is to forget one's own.
Abraham Lincoln

# DELUXE BREAD PUDDING

1 cups bread cubes
2 cups whole milk
3 Tbsp. butter
¼ cup sugar
2 eggs
a pinch of salt
½ tsp. vanilla

Cut day old bread into about ½"
square cubes. Turn into a small baking dish (qt. size). Mix milk, butter and
sugar. Heat just enough to melt butter and dissolve sugar. Beat eggs
slightly, add salt and then the warm
milk. Pour over bread. Set baking
dish in pan of hot water about 1"
deep. Bake in 325° oven for 1 hour or
until inserted knife in center comes
out clean.

**KITCHEN KAPERS:** If you are out of powdered
sugar, you can make your own. Add 1 Tbsp. of
cornstarch to 1 cup of white sugar. Blend in
blender until powdered. Yields 1½ cups.

# Helpful Hints
## For Making Freezer Ice Cream

To keep freezer ready, put it away freezer ready. Use your favorite recipe. Fill freezer can just below the lid mark. Adjust lid and crank handle. Some recipes will call for 8 parts of ice to 1 part of salt. One to six ratio seems reasonable to me.

Start with layer of ice in bottom of freezer, alternate layers of ice and salt until freezer bucket is full. Cover with newspaper or big towel. Pour water over ice and salt mixture to help start the ice to melt. Turn slowly the first 5-7 minutes. Then increase the speed until it becomes difficult to turn. When it comes to that stage, before removing the lid, take precaution to keep from getting salty water into the ice cream. Pour water over lid and wipe off; then remove the lid.

The next thing we did was remove the dasher, and the children had to "lick" the dasher. Then they were served 2 big bowls, before we packed to hold. Then we put the lid back on, plugged the hole in the lid with a twisted piece of paper towel.

We poured out the water from the freezer bucket, added more salt and ice, put the lid on, and let set for 2 hours before serving. We all had fun. My grandson and I do this every Summer when he visits me. Why don't we return to that nearly lost entertainment? There's nothing like making ice cream on the back porch or under a shade tree.

Use this recipe for your basic recipe for fruit juices or crushed fruit. Sweeten according to tartness of fruit.

## BASIC FREEZER ICE CREAM

2 cups sugar
¼ cup cornstarch
¼ tsp. salt
8 cups milk (whole or 2%)
4-6 eggs (beaten)
> 6 eggs will make it richer.

1 tall can evaporated milk
    (chill)
1 Tbsp. unflavored gelatin
> If using fruit, use the fruit flavor.

1½ tsp. vanilla

Mix sugar, cornstarch and salt in top of double boiler. Pour in 4 cups of milk gradually. Cook in double boiler, stir occasionally until thickens for about 4-6 minutes. Stir slowly a little of the cornstarch mixture into the beaten eggs. Then stir the egg mixture into the remaining cornstarch mixture. Cook over hot water for 4 or 5 minutes longer, stirring constantly. or until custard consistency. Soften gelatin into 1 cup of milk, then add to hot mixture. Chill thoroughly. This is essential to a smooth texture. When ready to put in freezer can, add remaining 3 cups of milk, evaporated milk and vanilla. Freeze 1 part salt to 6 parts ice.

# REFRIGERATOR
## VANILLA ICE CREAM

1 cup milk
1 Tbsp. cornstarch
½ cup sugar
a pinch of salt
1 egg yolk (beaten)
1 egg white
1 tsp. vanilla
2 cups coffee cream

Make a custard of first 5 ingredients. Cool and strain to get out the yolk anchors. I don't mind if they are left in, so I don't bother to strain. Whip egg whites until stiff. Whip coffee cream until foamy and add to egg whites. Fold into custard and add vanilla. Turn into refrigerator ice tray to freeze. Whip before it starts to freeze. If you will remove from tray and whip mixture with a wire whisk several times before freezing takes place, you will have the smoothest refrigerator cream I have ever seen. This is a good basic recipe to which fruit juices or crushed fruit can be added.

Calorie counters will appreciate this delicious milk.

# VANILLA ICE MILK

2 cups sugar
¼ cup cornstarch
¼ tsp. salt
8 cups (2 qts. skim milk)
3 eggs (beaten)
1 Tbsp. unflavored gelatine
1½ tsp. vanilla

Mix sugar, cornstarch, ¼ salt in top of double boiler. Blend in 4 cups skim milk gradually. Cook over hot water, stirring occasionally until thickens for about 12-15 minutes. Stir a little of the hot cornstarch mixture into the beaten eggs, then stir the eggs into the remaining cornstarch mixture. Cook over hot water and stir constantly, 4-5 minutes longer or until mixture is of the consistency of custard. Soften gelatin in 1 cup skim milk. Stir into hot mixture, chill thoroughly. This is very essential for a smooth ice milk. Stir in vanilla and the remaining 3 cups of skim milk. Pour into 1 gallon freezer, finish filling with skim milk just below the rim of lid, Freeze with 1 part salt to 6 parts ice.

These 2 recipes are to be made in refrigerator ice trays.

## PEACH SHERBET

1 cup evaporated milk
1 cup milk
1 cup water
1 Tbsp. lemon juice
2 cups peaches (mashed)
¼ cup sugar
¼ cup white Karo syrup
a pinch of salt

Mix and put into freezer tray. Remove when mixture is mushy and beat with wire whisk. Return to tray and whip twice more before freezing takes place.

## BUTTERMILK SHERBET

1 quart good fresh buttermilk
juice of 2 lemons
grated rind of another lemon
1 small can of pineapple
2½ cups sugar

Use the same instructions for Peach Sherbet.

# COOKIES
## AND
## CANDIES

Mike Allen and Sylvia Allen Worcester
Photograph by Marvin Allen

Aunt Lela was like our grandmother. She cooked for a family of 8 and made a home for them and my grandfather. She also roomed and boarded the teachers from a small rural school. Later, Aunt Lela moved to Denton, Texas, home of North Texas State Teachers College (as it was called then), and rented a boarding house in order for the three girls to go to college. She could make "something out of nothing."

## AUNT LELA'S TEA CAKES
the best ever

1 cup sugar
¼ cup butter
¼ cup lard
¼ tsp. salt
1½ cups flour
1 tsp. thick cream
1 egg
1 tsp. baking powder
1 tsp. vanilla

Sift and measure 1½ cups flour. Then add the salt and baking powder. Cream butter and lard. Add egg and vanilla. Beat thoroughly. Stir in flour mixture until dough can be handled easily. It helps to chill dough. Aunt Lela couldn't because of no refrigeration. Place on lightly floured board and roll out the desired thickness. Bake at 350° until light brown. Do not over cook. A thick cookie made a soft cookie. The thin and smaller cookie made a crisp cookie. Aunt Lela made the thick and large cookie about the size of a saucer. So good!

## KISSES
Jeannette Weaver

Beat egg whites until stiff, then beat in ½ cup of white sugar. Fold in ¾ cup of semi-sweet chocolate pieces. Add ¼ tsp. cream of tartar and 1 tsp. vanilla. Drop by rounded teaspoonfuls onto cookie sheets. Cover with heavy brown paper. Now we would use foil. Bake in 250° oven for 30-35 minutes or until Kisses are crisp to the touch. Cool and remove from cookie sheets with spatula.

This recipe for Peanut Butter Cookies belongs to Grace Allen, a sister-in-law of my husband. I have never heard an ill spoken word against her.

## PEANUT BUTTER COOKIES
in memory of Grace Allen

1 cup brown sugar
1 cup white sugar
1 cup Oleo 2 eggs (unbeaten)
1 cup peanut butter
1 cup flour (sifted) with
1 tsp. soda

Cream sugars and Oleo. Add rest in order given. Let dough chill. Then make into balls about the size of walnut. Mash into cookie shape by crisscrossing with a fork. Bake at 350° for 12-15 minutes.

# MARIE MILLS' OATMEAL COOKIES

Mix in order given:

2 cups granulated sugar
1 box brown sugar
1 lb. margarine
4 eggs (beaten)
1 small box (25¢) oatmeal (5
        cups, quick-cooking)
3 cups + scant ⅓ cup flour
        with salt
1 large package of chocolate
        chips
1½ Tbsp. salt
1½ Tbsp. soda

Add salt and baking soda to the flour. Add last 1 small box of quick-cooking oats and I large package of chocolate chips. This recipe makes a lot. You can freeze in rolls, slice and cook when needed. Bake at 350° for 10-12 minutes.

## EGGLESS COOKIES
Mrs. Gertrude Schrank
from Aunt Sue's 1927 P.T. A. cookbook

2 cups sugar
1 cup sweet milk
1 cup shortening
2 cups flour
1 tsp. vanilla

142

Cream shortening and sugar. Add milk and a pinch of salt. Sift and add dry ingredients and flavoring. Add more flour if needed to roll and cut out cookies. Cook in 350° oven until done. Do not over cook.

This recipe was given to me by Nancy Davis of Colquitt, Georgia. She says, "This recipe is special to me, for I was named after Aunt Mae (Amelia). I, in turn, passed the name on to my daughter Amelia Carol." – Nancy Amelia Widner Davis

## AUNT MAE'S TEA CAKES

1 cup sugar
2¾ cups plain flour
¾ cup butter
1 egg
1 tsp. soda
vanilla

Cream butter and sugar until fluffy. Add all other ingredients. Roll into rolls in wax paper for round cookies. This is also the recipe that I use when I want to use cookie cutters. Refrigerate dough for several hours before trying to work. Bake for about 10 minutes at 300°

I know this recipe has been used for several generations.

## AUNT LELA'S SOUR CREAM COOKIES

1 cup butter
2 cups light brown sugar
 2 eggs
¼ cup sour cream
3½ cups flour (sifted) to which
you add:
1 tsp. soda
1 tsp. cinnamon
1 tsp. cloves
1 tsp. nutmeg
½ cup pecans (chopped)
1 tsp. vanilla

Cream butter and sugar. Add 2 beaten eggs and ¼ cup of cream. You can use evaporated milk now. Sift and measure 3½ cups flour to which you add ½ tsp. soda and cinnamon, cloves and nutmeg. Add ½ cups pecans and vanilla. Drop by tsp. or roll in walnut size ball and mash with glass. Bake at 350°. Do not over cook.

Fern Tims was a dear friend of mine; her parents and my husband's family were life long friends. Both moved to Jackson County, Oklahoma, from Decatur, Texas. She was a patron of mine for over 35 years. If you remember, Marvin and I operated a beauty shop for over 50 years.

## EASY DATE COOKIES
in memory of Fern Tims

1 cup shortening (½ cup and ½ cup Crisco)
2 cups brown sugar
2 eggs
½ cup water
1 tsp. vanilla
3½ cups flour
½ tsp. salt
1 tsp. soda (scant)

Cream shortening and sugar. Add eggs one at at time. Beat after each addition. Stir in water and vanilla. Add soda, salt and cinnamon to flour and add to cream mixture. Drop tsp. of dough on ungreased cookie sheet. Place tsp. date filling on dough, then top with ½ tsp. dough. Bake until light brown, 10-12 minutes at 400°.

Date filling:
2 cups dates (chopped)
¾ cups water
½ cup nuts

Cook together slowly, stirring until thick. Add nuts when dates are cooked. Cool slightly before adding to dough.

# SUGAR COOKIES
Minnie Furr
a friend of Aunt Sue
recipe handwritten in Aunt Sue's bank
deposit book

2 cups sugar
1 cup shortening
1 cup sour cream
2 eggs
1 tsp. vanilla
4½ cups flour (sifted)

Mix ingredients and add to dry ingredients. Raisins, coconut or nuts may be added if desired. Roll thin and cut. Bake about 10-12 minutes.

The older the recipes, the less mixing instructions are included. The explanation – everybody in that era was introduced to cooking; thus detailed instructions were not necessary.

# PINEAPPLE COOKIES
Olivia Robinson

½ cup butter
½ cup brown sugar
½ cup granulated sugar
½ cup pineapple (drained and crushed)
½ cup nuts (chopped)
1 egg (well beaten)
¼ tsp. salt
¼ tsp. soda
1 tsp. baking powder
1 tsp. vanilla

Cream shortening with sugar. Add egg and pineapple. Mix thoroughly and add vanilla. Sift flour and measure and sift with baking powder, soda and salt. Add nuts. Mix well. Drop by tsp. on a greased cookie sheet in 350° oven for about 10-12 minutes.

## OATMEAL COOKIES
in memory of Floyd Robinson

1¼ sticks butter
¼ + ⅛ cup brown sugar
¼ cup white sugar
1 egg
1 cup flour
1½ cup oats
½ tsp. vanilla
½ tsp. cinnamon
½ tsp. soda
½ tsp. salt

Mix well and form into balls about 1 tsp. amount or a little more. Bake 375° for 10 minutes. Makes 2¼ dozen.

Spoon Holders
photograph by Michael Allen

147

Jack Sides was a neighbor of Aunt Sue and Uncle Ennis He couldn't have been better to his own mother. Uncle Ennis died several years before Aunt Sue died. He took care of their every need just perfectly. She loved him like a son.

Those early recipes had very little instructions. Everybody cooked and didn't need instructions. This is Jack Sides' mother's recipe, handwritten by Aunt Sue. This is the recipe verbatim.

## TEA CAKES

1 cup sugar
½ cup butter
6 Tbsp. milk
2 eggs
1½ tsp. vanilla
1 tsp. baking powder

In a P. S. Aunt Sue has written, "Add enough flour to make a stiff dough to roll." If you want a crisp cookie, roll thin and small. If a thick and soft cookie is preferred, roll thick and large. Bake 350° until light brown on edges. Don't over cook.

## AUNT SUE'S SOUTHERN PRALINES
circa 1954

This recipe is done in 4 steps.
Step 1:
Combine 2 cups sugar and 1 tsp. soda in a deep 3 quart saucepan. Mix well. Use wooden spoon to stir.

Add 1 cup light cream. Now you would use half & half cream. Stir carefully to keep sugar in crystals in bottom of pan. All sugar should be dissolved when candy boils.

Step 2:
Bring to boil over medium heat, stirring only enough to keep from scorching. When it starts to boil, it will bubble high. Reduce heat and keep stirring to keep from boiling over. It will caramelize slightly as it cooks. Cook to a soft ball stage or 234° by a candy thermometer. If you don't have one, they are a good investment and don't cost much. Test several times.

Step 3:
Remove from heat. Add exactly 1½ Tbsp. butter. Too much butter will keep candy from firming. Add 2 cups pecan halves. Beat mixture until thick Drop from a spoon (metal is best). Candy will get thick rapidly.

Step 4:
Drop candy on a wax paper or lightly buttered foil. A large cookie sheet works well. Set aside to cool.

George Starks loved to make peanut brittle and was well known for it. He made a lot of it and gave much of it away. He was the manager of the J. C. Penny store in Altus, Oklahoma, for years. But to him his most important work was being an Elder for many years in the Elm and Hudson Church of Christ, where I have attended for over 64 years.

## PEANUT BRITTLE
### in memory of George Starks

2 cups sugar
1 cup white Karo syrup
¾ cup water
2 cups raw peanuts (heaping)
2 tsp. soda
2 tsp. vanilla
2 level Tbsp. butter
a scant tsp. of salt

Boil the first 3 ingredients until it spins a thread or makes a brittle ball when tested in cold water about 15-20 minutes from the start of actual cooking. Add peanuts and scant tsp. of salt. Cook until syrup turns a deep tan color. Add soda, butter and vanilla. Stir well and pour on cookie sheets. I still use a 50 year old Maytag stove (tabletop), so I pour the candy on the top between the burners. Pour fast and spread evenly. As soon as it cools enough, pull from the edges with fingers and stretch as thin as possible, work toward the center.

The center is the hottest. It's best when pulled very thin. The outer edges will begin to break as you work toward the center. When you have pulled all of it, break in uneven pieces. I tap it with a knife handle. Wait about 3 hours, until well cooled, before covering it. It's lower in calories than the cream candies. It keeps good, if you hide it.

This is a good Christmas candy, but it's good anytime. When my sister and I were growing up, making candy was great entertainment when we had our girl friends stay all night with us.

## MRS. MILLS CREAMY CANDY

4 cups sugar
1½ cups dark corn syrup
1 pint. cream
1 cup pecans

Boil syrup, sugar and cream together until forms a soft ball. Let cool to luke-warm, then reheat over hot water until creamy. Add nuts, turn out on a buttered platter and knead. Mold in a loaf for slicing.

# CANDIED ORANGE PEEL
old recipe

Peel, but leave as much of the white part as possible. Cut the rind off in narrow strips and then cut in small parts with scissors, cover with cold water and bring to a boil and boil about 5 minutes. Repeat boiling and pour off water four or five times to get rid of the bitter oils in the rind. Make a syrup by using twice as much sugar as you use water – that is 2 cups sugar to 1 cup water. The amount of syrup you use depends upon the amount of fruit you have.

Put peel in syrup and boil until peel is clear and is boiled down real clear. It should be clear by now. Dip peel out of pan and roll in powdered sugar. Put on pan to cool and dry out. Make sure they are thoroughly dry so peel won't stick together. Lemon and grapefruit can be prepared the same way.

This was a favorite confection in days past and was used in fruitcakes, cookies, breads, or rolls.

I have made this fudge for over 60 years, and if I write 10 more cookbooks, it will be in all 10.

## OLD TIMEY FUDGE

2 cups sugar

¾ cup of top milk (the cream
    that rises to the top)
    You could use about ½ cup regular
    milk and ¼ cup evaporated milk to
    make ¾ cup of milk. Finish filling the
    cup with white Karo syrup.

½ cup cocoa (or less)

1 tsp. vanilla

2 Tbsp. butter

Rub the rim of a thick heavy skillet with butter to prevent the candy mixture from boiling over. Mix sugar, milk, syrup, and cocoa. Stir until sugar is dissolved. Increase heat and do not stir again. When it forms a soft ball in cold water, add butter and vanilla. Set aside for about 20 minutes until cooled. Do not disturb. Beat until thickened and heavy enough to stand along when pulled up. Put in a well buttered pan. Cut in squares.

**KITCHEN KAPERS:** If fudge gets too stiff before you can get it into a pan, knead with buttered hands until creamy and press into pan.

# AUNT SUE'S DATE LOAF CANDY
circa 1939

1 cup sugar
2 Tbsp. corn syrup
1 cup water
3 Tbsp. butter
1 cup dates (chopped)
⅛ tsp. salt
1 cup pecan halves

Cook sugar, corn syrup, water, and butter to soft ball stage. Add dates and cook until they are cooked up. You can mash dates on the side of the skillet with a wooden spoon. Remove from heat, stir in salt and unbroken pecans into candy, stir very lightly. Pour on a damp linen cloth and make into a firm roll. You rarely find linen, so I used a cup towel made from a flour sack. (If we were embroidering them, my mother bought unbleached muslin for 5 cents a yard or sometimes 2 yards for 5 cents.) When cold remove from cloth and slice thin. Eat to your heart's content, then take an hour to walk, jog or run.

# CHRISTMAS DIVINITY
Marie Mills

3 cups sugar
¾ cup white Karo syrup
¾ cup water
1 pkg. Strawberry Jell-O
2 egg whites
½ cup pecans

Cook sugar, syrup and water to a soft ball stage. Beat egg whites until frothy. Then add Jell-O. Continue beating until very stiff. Pour egg whites into first mixture in a very small stream. Beat until it begins to thicken. Add nuts. Coconut may be added. This is when it begins to harden really fast. Drop on wax paper by tsp. full.

# BEST PEANUT BUTTER FUDGE
Jeannette Weaver

2-3 cups sugar
1 cup milk
1 stick butter
1 cup peanut butter (plain or
        crunchy)
a pinch of salt
1 tsp. vanilla

Boil together until forms a soft ball in a cup of cold water. Beat by hand until thick. Take off heat. Add vanilla after it cools. Pour onto platter and cut in squares when cool.

I was told by Lou Kerr, daughter-in-law of the late Senator Robert S. Kerr of Oklahoma, that Aunt Bill was a relative of the Kerr family. I don't know the age of this recipe, but I do know that it won First Prize in county fairs and nut shows every time it was entered. It was given to me every Christmas by Betty Vaniman, beginning in the '40s until she died in the '70s. I guess it would have to be my favorite. It's possible for 1 person to make it, but you really need two people.

## AUNT BILL'S BROWN CANDY
### in memory of Betty Vaniman

3 pints granulated sugar
¼ lb. butter
1 tsp. vanilla
1 pint cream or whole milk
¼ tsp. soda
2 lbs. pecans

Put 1 pint sugar in heavy skillet, preferable iron, but aluminum will work. Place under low heat and start stirring immediately with a wooden spoon. Keep the sugar moving constantly to keep it from scorching. Never let it smoke or cook so fast that it will turn dark. It should be the color of light brown syrup. The caramelizing of the sugar should take about 30 minutes.

Put into another deep heavy pan the rest of the cream or milk and set over low heat. Let it cook slowly while you are caramelizing the sugar in the skillet. As soon as the caramelized, start pouring it in the kettle of boiling milk. This is where you need the second person. Pour sugar in a very thin stream. Keep on very low fire and stir constantly. This is the secret of mixing these ingredients – the low heat and thin stream. Continue cooking and stirring until mixture forms a firm ball when dropped into a cup of cold water. Then turn off heat and add soda. Stir vigorously as it foams up. Now add the butter. Now set it off the stove for about 20 minutes. Do not set it outside or in a cold place. Wait about 20 minutes. Now add vanilla and begin beating. Use a wooden spoon until the mixture is thick and heavy and loses its gloss. Add broken pecans and mix. When slightly cooled, pour into square pans, so it can be cut into squares. This candy will stay moist, I guess forever, enabling you to make it early for Christmas.

# SAUCEPAN PRALINES

1 cup granulated sugar
1 cup light brown sugar
    (packed)
½ cup water
¼ cup light corn syrup
1 tsp. salt
1 tsp. vanilla
1 Tbsp. vinegar
1 – 6 oz. pkg. of butterscotch
    morsels
3 cups coarsely chopped
    pecans
1 tsp. vanilla

Combine in sauce pan sugars, water, syrup, salt, and mix well. Turn to highest control and bring mixture to a rolling boil. The instant the mixture boils, turn off heat, but leave on burner. Let stand 3 minutes without a lid. Do not stir. Then add morsels, vanilla and pecans. Stir until morsels are dissolved. Drop quickly by teaspoonfuls on wax paper. Yields 5½ dozen (2-2½ inches diameter.)

Nova Crow obtained this recipe when her son was stationed in the armed forces in Louisiana many years ago. She brought food to my house on just about every occasion (weddings, funerals and Christmas), or "just to be doing." She was a wonderful cook.

## NOVA CROW'S
## PECAN PRALINES
in memory of Nova Crow

2 cups white sugar
1 tsp. soda
a pinch of salt
   the amount you can hold between
   finger and thumb
1 cup buttermilk
2 Tbsp. butter
   measure carefully, too much will
   keep it from creaming.
2-3 cups pecans

In a large heavy saucepan, mix sugar, soda, buttermilk, and salt. Boil over high heat for 5 minutes or until reaches 210° on candy thermometer. If you don't have one, now is a good time to buy one. Stir frequently scraping the bottom and sides of pan to prevent sticking. Cook until reaches soft ball stage or 234° or about 5 minutes. Remove from heat and cool slightly. Beat until thick and creamy. Drop from tablespoon onto wax paper. Yields 16-18 (2 inch) pralines.

# MARY ALICE'S PEANUT PATTIES
a friend of Fern Tims

Boil:
2½ cups sugar
⅔ cup of white syrup
1 cup milk
3 cups raw peanuts

Cook until forms a firm ball in cold water. Then add:

1 Tbsp. butter
a few drops of red food coloring

Beat by hand until hard enough to drop on wax paper by spoonfuls.

Mike and Sylvia can't remember when we didn't have this cookie jar.
Photograph by Michael Allen

# BREADS

**Old Timey Thresher**
photograph by Michael Allen

# The Staff Of Life

Bread in the early days was truly "the staff of life." It should be today, but we have the notion it's fattening. It really isn't, if we eat it in moderation and leave off those fattening spreads. Bread is so nourishing and satisfying.

Bread was our snacks when we came home from school – a cold biscuit with a fresh onion from the garden or a biscuit with holes punched in it, filled with sorghum. My father in his later years was a small produce trucker and hauled sorghum from Sulpher Springs, Texas. He taught our children to pour sorghum over ice cream. They still like it.

The average family used 50-75 gallons of sorghum a year for cooking cakes, cookies, candies, and many other things. There was always a big bowl of butter on the table and a syrup pitcher of Mary Jane Corn Syrup, if not sorghum. The labels had a doll on it similar to Sunbonnet Sue with blue and white checks or pink and white checks for the dress and bonnet, depending on the contents of the half gallon bucket. One color labeled the dark and one labeled the white syrup. We tried so hard to get the labels off the bucket without tearing. They were in great demand for paper dolls. Aunt Lela saved them for us. She was like a grandmother to us. She was 16 and the eldest of eight children with the youngest being 5 months old when my Grandma Bonds died. She and my Grandfather made a home for those children. She never married and continued to make a home for her and Grandfather Bonds as long as he lived. So we would go to Grandpa and Aunt Lela's.

We always had hot biscuits for breakfast. We would cut the biscuit open with a table knife which would heat the knife and the butter would slide off the knife before we could get it in the biscuit. We learned to fan the knife while the butter was being passed to us. Somehow I feel sorry for people who have never had the privilege of eating those hot homemade fluffy buttermilk biscuits with the homemade sorghum drenched with the fresh churned butter. We had never heard of cholesterol or calories. It made no difference because we worked from daylight until dark and worked it off. We never knew the word, "bored." No doubt if we'd used it our parents would have soon put us to work.

One of the crops we raised was wheat. We only had 60 acres in cultivation with a part of it in wheat. That was all 1 family could take care of with a planter, cultivator and a harrow pulled by a team of horses. We would bind the wheat into bundles by machinery and stack it by hand. It was dried for awhile and then was ready for the thresher. It was a thrill to see the steam thresher with its big smokestack. My sister and I could hear it coming, and we would stand on a bale of hay at the gate. Standing on the bale made us taller, so we could see the thresher coming. There was an expression, "Sounds like a threshing machine," and that thresher did. We didn't have to feed the thresher crew. They had their own cook wagon. One year my father cooked for the thresher crew that came to work in our area. He told them he couldn't cook desserts, but he cooked gallons of potatoes and beans, salt pork, corn bread, and dried fruit. The cook wagon had a table made of a 1"x12" plank that pulled down, and they stood up to eat. Every crew member had his own bedroll and by the time their day was over, I'm sure they were ready to "hit the hay." The thresher and crew would stay in our community for about 3 or 4 weeks. My brother, Charlie, took our wagon and team and hauled bundles of wheat to the trasher for hire. We raised enough wheat to take it to the mill and turn it into flour, and some to sell and some to keep for seed.

After we left the farm near Mineral Wells, Texas, in 1928, we moved to Blair, Oklahoma. In six months my mother was killed in a tornado. My parents both had small businesses that were lost in the storm from which we were not able to "comeback." Then the Great Depression hit. I've learned since then that there were some welfare programs. My father never thought the World owed him a living; I suppose he was too proud to call for help. We survived without it. In the middle of The Depression, my father traded a milk cow for a truck, and things began to look up for us. I don't know what he traded for the cow.

This recipe dates back to about 1920. It was written down in my Aunt Sue's bank deposit book dated in 1920. Everybody used this method of making "light bread" as it was called then. We made it all the time during the Summer, because the yeast worked better in the hot weather, and we didn't have to build a fire in the cookstove to make bread every day that heated the kitchen.

## AUNT SUE'S EVERLASTING YEAST STARTER

1 cup flour
½ cup sugar

Add enough warm water to make a stiff batter. Pour in a fruit jar with loose lid. Set in a warm place out of a draft until it's light and foamy. This will take 5-10 days. Once you get it working for you, it will last for years.

Yeast cakes or dry yeast is so much simpler and was available according to this excerpt from a pamphlet printed prior to Oklahoma statehood.

"Fleischman's yeast is a plant which needs warmth, air and moisture to grow. It is killed by an excess of heat or cold. Anything too warm for hand is too warm for yeast and anything that chills the yeast will stop its growth. For this reason all liquids should be lukewarm and the flour should also be warmed in the winter. Our yeast contains pure tapioca flour to better sustain it's natural quality in distribution and taste. Guaranteed by The Fleischman Company under the Food and Drugs Act, June 30, 1906."

This recipe is made with Aunt Sue's everlasting yeast. The directions in that era were not very plain. They didn't have to be, because everybody knew how to cook. Even the children knew how, because they watched their mother and grandmothers cook standing on a chair or a wooden box.

## LIGHT BREAD
as it was called then

Mix 1 quart of water with 1 cup of everlasting yeast, saved over from last baking, with enough flour to make a fairly stiff batter. Mix at 4pm in the Summer or noon in the Winter. Let rise until night. Punch down, work into dough and set overnight. (When they said work into dough, that means add as much flour as needed.) Next morning, punch down, knead dough thoroughly, mold, let rise until double in size. Bake in moderate oven.

## HOW TO KNEAD YEAST DOUGH

Punch down in center. Lay on floured board. Use more flour if needed to handle. Pull with forefinger the dough to center and then work with the heel of your hand, sinking into dough. Let the heel do the work. Don't be in a hurry. Repeat until the dough is elastic and smooth for 10 - 15 minutes.

This is good to know when learning the art of making the early day bread.

Sometimes you'll learn you don't have enough batter to take out for your next recipe and still leave 1 cup for your mother yeast. Then you have to build up your starter. This is how it is done.

## HOW TO KEEP AND USE
## STARTER

To 1 cup of starter that is working, add 2 cups of warm potato water (or just warm water), 2 Tbsp. sugar and 2½ cups of flour, or enough to make a medium batter. This will make 1 quart of batter. You'll need to build this up the day before you plan to use it. In real hot weather, the heat forms too much acid and will destroy itself in 2 or 3 days, and it had to be built up every day. With air-conditioned days, you only have to build it up the day before you plan to use it.

Good luck to you in learning the now forgotten art of making your own yeast. It's real satisfying and very rewarding. Your family will love you for it.

In making yeast mixture, it should never be too hot or too cold, always lukewarm. My mother would warm the flour in Winter. Thank goodness, that is not necessary now. Our houses were so cold and drafty that we slept under no telling how many heavy quilts, in long handle underwear and maybe a hot rock by our feet. It was wrapped in paper or good parts of cotton-picking sacks. We also made towels from the sacks for the men to dry their hands on when they were doing dirty work before dinner (noon).

## RULES FOR MAKING YEAST DOUGH

1. Mix milk, salt, sugar, and shortening, dissolve yeast in a little milk mixture. Beat until smooth.

2. Now you are ready to add flour – the amount your recipe calls for, or enough to make a stiff dough. Set in a warm place to let rise until double in size.

3. Punch down and knead on a well-floured dough board and add more flour if needed to make a dough to handle.

4. Put in a big mixing bowl well-greased and turn so that all sides are greased. Let rise until double in size and punch down.

5. Cut off dough in right size to make whatever you want.

6. Let rise again until double in size. Bake at 375° about 45 minutes. Rolls will bake in less time.

167

This recipe is from a P. T.A. cookbook dated in 1927 that belonged to my Aunt Sue when she lived in London, Texas.

## ICEBOX YEAST BREAD
Mrs. G.W. Vierling, Sr.

Mix 2 cups of boiling water, ½ cup of sugar to 1 Tbsp. salt, 2 Tbsp. shortening (melted shortening, but don't get it hot or will kill the yeast). Let cool to lukewarm. Soften 2 cakes of compressed yeast in ¼ cup of lukewarm water. Add 1 tsp. sugar and stir into first mixture. Add 2 beaten eggs and stir in 3 or 4 cups of flour and beat thoroughly. But do not knead. Cover and put in icebox to have on hand. When ready to use, shape into loaves or light rolls. Let rise 3 or 4 hours before you wish to bake. The special advantage of this dough is that it need not be used at once. Simply take out what is needed and return remainder to icebox. This was before the days of electric refrigeration.

# SOUR DOUGH STARTER

1 cake of yeast
or
1 package of dry yeast
dissolved in
4 cups water
or 2 pints of warm water
2 Tbsp. sugar
4 cups flour
1 raw potato (cut in fourths)

Mix all ingredients in a crock and let rise until very light and slightly aged. The time required for ageing depends on the temperature. If the weather is real hot, it will be ready in 10-12 days. If it's cold weather it will take longer to become ready for use. When it's light and bubbly it is ready for use. The water will rise to the top if the sponge gets too sour and will keep it from rising properly. To keep this from happening, add a little sugar every few days.

A slice of bread with a moderate spread of butter will give you more energy than a candy bar.

# JUST PLAIN YEAST BREAD
with white flour, made into loaves

2 pkgs. yeast (I prefer Red Star brand)
1½ cups lukewarm water
1½ cups milk (scalded and cooled)
3 Tbsp. sugar
3 Tbsp. lard or melted butter
7½ cups flour (about)
1½ tsp. of salt

Dissolve yeast and sugar in lukewarm liquid. Then add lard or butter. Then add gradually flour, enough to make a stiff dough that you can handle easily. Add salt to flour. Knead thoroughly, be sure to keep dough soft. Then place into a greased bowl. Make sure all sides are greased. Let rise until double in size in a warm place. Place on floured board. Work slightly; shape into loaves and let rise about an hour. Put folded edge on the bottom of pan. Bake at 350° for about an hour. Yields 2 loaves.

Pauline Brown is a retired home economist from Lone Wolf, Oklahoma. She is in her middle eighties, and half of Lone Wolf uses this recipe. She taught lots of young girls the art of cooking; one of them being Janell Woolsey who gave me this recipe. Thanks to Pauline for her contribution to society.

## EVERLASTING ROLLS
### Pauline Brown

Dissolve 1 cake yeast in ½ cup luke-warm water. Add ½ tsp. sugar. Let stand 30-45 minutes. Cream together ½ cup sugar and ½ cup shortening. And 1 egg and beat. To this add 1 cup milk poured into 1 cup hot water and 1½ tsp. salt. Cool to lukewarm and add enough flour to make a stiff batter and beat until smooth (about 7½ cups). Add enough flour to make a soft dough (of flour in all) and knead until smooth. Cover and let rise in a warm place until double in size. A warm room temperature is best, not where dough will get hot. Shape and place in well-greased pans and let rise again until double in bulk. Bake in 425° oven for 15-20 minutes. They lend themselves to any shape desired such as Parker House, Cloverleaf, Bow Knot or cinnamon rolls.

For cinnamon rolls, roll dough out to ¼" thick. Cover with softened Oleo, sprin-kle with sugar, cinnamon and raisins, if preferred. Roll and slice. Lay flat in pan and let rise. Dough can be stored in the refrigerator for several days.

This recipe was used by the cowboys. The advantage was they didn't need milk, called for very little oil and baked nicely in the dutch oven. It was said that they took the starter to bed with them. They were real cowboys not the "drugstore" variety.

## SOUR DOUGH BISCUITS

Form a nest of sifted flour – about 2 cups. Pour about 2 cups of starter in nest. Sprinkle over the sponge ½ tsp. salt, 1 Tbsp. sugar, 2 heaping Tbsp. baking powder. Mix to a soft dough. Turn out on a board and pat or roll ½" thick. Bake in a well-greased iron skillet. Grease top of biscuits, cover and set in a warm place out of a draft. Let rise about 15 minutes and bake in a very hot pre-heated oven 474° - 500° until golden brown.

## SWEET MILK ROLLS
Mrs. Coke R. Stephenson
from Aunt Sue's P.T. A. cookbook

1 cup sweet milk heated to warmth of fresh milk. Divide, to 1 part add 1 cake of Fleischman yeast, to other part add 1 tsp. salt, ½ cup melted Crisco, 2 Tbsp. sugar. Mix together both liquids. Mix to soft dough. Turn out on floured board. Knead 20 minutes by the clock. Grease over the top with melted Crisco. Let rise 2 hours and bake in moderate oven for 20 minutes.

# AUNT SUE'S
# BAKING POWDER BISCUITS
circa 1920

2 cups flour
2 tsp. baking powder
¾ tsp. salt
1 tsp. sugar

> when you use sweet milk, you need sugar to make it brown. Buttermilk with about ¼ tsp. soda will brown better and will be more flaky.

4 Tbsp. shortening
about ¾ cup milk

Mix flour with baking powder, sugar and salt. Cut in shortening with pastry blender until mixture is like coarse meal. Add milk and stir quickly with a fork until the mixture forms a soft ball that will follow the fork without sticking to the side of the bowl. You'll need about 2 minutes to add the liquid. Turn dough out on a lightly floured cloth covered board. White ducking makes a good cloth. Knead about 30 seconds. Pat gently to about ½" sheet. Cut with a floured cutter. They will brown better on a cookie sheet, bake about 12 minutes in a 450° oven.

**KITCHEN KAPERS:** 1 tsp. baking powder can be made from ½ tsp. cream of tartar and ¼ tsp. baking soda.

# EASY ROLLS
quick

¾ cup scalded milk
½ cup sugar
1 tsp. salt
½ stick Oleo
½ cup water (lukewarm)
2 packages yeast
1 egg
3½ cups flour

Scald milk and stir in butter, sugar and salt. Cool to lukewarm. Measure water in bowl, sprinkle in yeast and stir. Beat egg into milk mixture and add 2 cups of the flour. Beat until smooth. Stir in rest of flour. Cover. Let rise until double in bulk. Punch down, knead and shape into rolls. Let rise 30 minutes. Bake at 350° for about 15 minutes. Yields 2 dozen small rolls.

I remember when we first married, my sister-in-law, Zora Baker, made a spread for hot biscuits with dried apricots and a can of crushed pineapple, cooked until the right consistency to spread. She also taught me to serve peanut butter mixed with white Karo syrup spread on a buttered biscuit. Both are very good and satisfying.

**KITCHEN KAPERS:** 1 cup self-rising flour can be made from all purpose flour by adding ½ tsp. soda and 1 tsp. baking powder.

I kept having calls for the sweet potato biscuit. Most of the calls were coming from the Deep South. So finally I found this recipe. It's an old one from Mississippi, and I was really happy to find it.

## SWEET POTATO BISCUIT

1½ cup all purpose flour
4 tsp. baking powder
½ tsp. salt
2 Tbsp. sugar
½ cup shortening
¼ cup milk
1¼ cup mashed sweet potatoes

Mix all dry ingredients. Cut in shortening until mixture is coarse like meal. Combine milk and sweet potato. Blend into flour mixture. Roll out and cut into biscuits ½" thick. Bake at 425° for about 15 minutes.

## POTATO SPLIT BISCUITS
### Minnie Hall
from Aunt Sue's P.T. A. cookbook

2 large Irish potatoes boiled or baked. When cool enough to handle, add 1 cup shortening, melted to lukewarm (now we have liquid oil) to the potatoes, ½ tsp. salt, 1 tsp. sugar, 2 well-beaten eggs, 1 qt. flour, and 1 cup warm milk to dissolve ½ cake of yeast in. Let rise and add 2 cups flour. Roll to cut out with biscuit cutter. and divide into halves. Spread with melted butter. Cut out the other half and place on on top of the other. Let rise and cook quickly.

175

Minnie White was a dear friend, as well as our house-keeper, my children's baby sitter during the week and a Bible teacher on Sunday. She lived to be almost 99 years old. This is her biscuit recipe.

## BUTTERMILK BISCUITS
in memory of Minnie White

2 cups flour
½ tsp. salt
4 tsp. baking powder
½ tsp. baking soda (scant)
5 Tbsp. shortening
1 cup sour milk

Mix flour, salt, soda, and baking powder. Cut in shortening until mixture resembles coarse crumbs. Add milk and stir with fork until follows fork around bowl. Turn out on floured board, knead ½ minute, roll and cut. Bake on an ungreased sheet about 12-15 minutes at 450°.

## HOW TO TOAST BREAD

Arrange slices of bread (day old bread works best) or split leftover muffins on broiler rack. I put the bread on foil. Run under a broiler unit until lightly toasted. Remove, turn slices, brush generously with melted butter. Return to oven and toast a golden brown. Serve immediately.

**KITCHEN KAPERS:** 1 cup sifted cake flour can be made from 1 cup sifted all purpose flour minus 2 Tbsp. flour plus 1 Tbsp. cornstarch.

This Kush recipe was another way to use leftover bread in the pioneer days. The men were especially fond of it. It was nourishing, too.

## KUSH

leftover corn bread
Sometimes a leftover baking
powder biscuit might be cut up
with the corn bread.

1 or 2 tsp. butter to each slice
of corn bread
milk

Melt the butter in a heavy sauce pan or skillet. Cut corn bread into chunks and add the melted butter. Turn over a little bit, being careful not to break the chunks. Pour in a little milk and stir again lightly. Cover with a lid and let set for a minute. Serve from a bowl. Eat with a fork like spoon bread.

## HUSH PUPPIES
in memory of my Aunt Sue

2 cups meal
1 tsp. flour
1 cup milk or water
1 tsp. salt
2 tsp. baking powder
½ cup onion (chopped, fine)
1 egg, if desired
1 tsp. butter (melted} or bacon
drippings

Shape in small pones, fry in deep, hot fat until good and brown.

# BASIC PANCAKE BATTER
We called them hot cakes.

2 cups flour
3 tsp. baking powder
¼ tsp. salt
2½ Tbsp. sugar
2 eggs (beaten)
1 cup milk
2 Tbsp. butter (melted)

Combine dry ingredients, blend milk and beaten eggs and add melted butter. Add milk mixture to dry ingredients. Stir only enough to blend. Pancakes will be better if batter is slightly bumpy. Grease with very little oil when skillet is hot. Drop by spoonfuls or pour batter from pitcher to form 4 or 5 inch rounds. Of course, now we have those wonderful nonstick skillets. I cook one at a time. That seems to be all I can handle. Cook until it's full of bubbles. I reduce heat when I first put batter in skillet. When full of bubbles, turn and cook until the other side is slightly brown. To vary the flavor fold in ⅓ cup of blueberries, bananas or fruit of your choice. Serve with syrup while hot, drenched with melted butter.

**KITCHEN KAPERS:** For lighter pancakes or waffles, replace the liquid with club soda and non-fat dry instant milk.

# BUTTERMILK PANCAKES

Use basic batter but substitute buttermilk for sweet milk. Use 1 tsp. baking powder and add ¼ tsp. baking soda. I use 1 Tbsp. sugar. The sugar helps it brown nicely. Cook and serve like the basic pancake. You can cover and refrigerate and use at your convenience.

My brother-in-law, Tom Allen operated a cafe during the Depression, and this was his syrup recipe that was good and cheap to make.

## MY FAVORITE PANCAKE SYRUP
in memory of Tom Allen

1 cup brown sugar
1 cup granulated sugar
1 cup water a pinch of salt
1 tsp. Maplelene flavor

Mix ingredients. Let come to a boil. Add maplelene flavor and let set until cool. Put in a syrup pitcher. Everybody had a syrup pitcher with an aluminum lid and handle.

**KITCHEN KAPERS:** To separate bacon from container, remove the very outside container, roll from end to end, making a cylinder. This will separate the pieces and make it easier to put in pan.

# Waffles

When Marvin and I were first married we went to the Jackson County Fair, Altus, Oklahoma, and won a waffle iron. It was great. I'd never seen one before. Remember, we were still in the Depression Days. When we married, Marvin had a "hole in the wall" barber shop with a beauty shop in the back. He was self-taught, and it didn't take me long to pick up the beauty trade. So we had a little money coming in. We did O.K. We couldn't save money, but we were able to pay the rent, have a telephone and buy a 2-tray Kelvinator refrigerator (electric). We could buy round steak, enough for three meals for 25 cents, and you could also buy a big roast for 75 cents. We had to gross $5 a day to live modestly and pay living expenses to survive – no luxuries. But we were thankful for that!

I still have the waffle iron we won at the county fair and still use it occasionally. This next recipe came with the iron.

photograph by Michael Allen

# PECAN WAFFLES

2 eggs
2 cups buttermilk
¼ tsp. baking soda
2 cups flour (sifted)
2 tsp. baking powder
½ tsp. salt
2 Tbsp. soft shortening
½ - 1 cup pecans (chopped)

Beat eggs and milk together well. Sift together flour, soda, baking powder, and salt. Beat into egg mixture. Stir in shortening and pecans. Cook in hot waffle iron. The waffle iron had no control, so cook to a golden brown. Serve with butter, syrup or preserves. So good and crisp!

My mother taught Marie and me how to make this simple recipe for corn bread for our dinner (noon meal). We always made this corn bread on wash day and ironing day. The real Southern corn bread did not have sugar or flour.

# CORN BREAD

2 cups buttermilk
1 egg
1 tsp. salt
½ tsp. soda (scant)
3 Tbsp. baking powder
2 cups corn meal
2½ Tbsp. cooking oil
We used bacon drippings.

Put 2 cups buttermilk in mixing bowl. Add salt, soda, baking powder. Beat in egg and add oil. Add meal to liquid mixture. While mixing bread, put about 1 Tbsp. of oil in skillet and get it really hot, but not smoking. Bake in oven 450° - 475°. Don't forget the butter. Why not serve with black-eyed peas?

181

Mike Freels vows this is the only way to make corn bread.

## CORN BREAD
## KENTUCKY STYLE
Mike Freels
Henderson, Kentucky

4 cups white meal
1½ cups all-purpose flour
2-4 Tbsp. sugar
1½ tsp. soda
4 tsp. baking powder
2 tsp. salt
½ cup oil
4 eggs

Mix all dry ingredients together. Add milk, eggs and oil to dry ingredients. Mix well. Bake at 350° in black iron skillet for 25-30 minutes. Get the oil in skillet to smoking.

## BANANA NUT BREAD
makes 4 loaves

2 sticks Oleo (margarine)
2 cups sugar
4 eggs
6 bananas (mashed, real
    ripe a must)
1 tsp. salt
2 tsp. soda
4 cups flour
2 tsp. vanilla
½ cup nuts

Cream Oleo and sugar. Beat in eggs. Add mashed bananas. Blend well. Add salt and soda to flour. Add vanilla and nuts. Turn into greased and floured loaf pans. Bake at 350° for 1 hour. If you want a moist crust, wrap in foil, while hot. Let cool before freezing or eat immediately. It will mold if not eaten in a few days.

This recipe was handwritten by Aunt Sue in her 1927 P.T.A. cookbook.

## NUT BREAD

1½ cups sugar
1 Tbsp. lard
1 tsp. salt
2 eggs
2 cups sweet milk
2 cups white flour
2 cups graham flour
4 tsp. baking powder
1 cup ground raisins
1 cup nuts (chopped)

Cream the sugar and shortening. Add beaten eggs. Sift and measure the flour, then add salt and baking powder. Add flour and milk alternately beginning with flour and ending with flour. Bake in moderate oven 45 - 60 minutes or until done. Makes 2 loaves. Good for lunches and brunches. Serve with hot butter.

**KITCHEN KAPERS:** If you have overripe bananas and no time to bake banana bread, mash just the right amount for your recipe and freeze for future use.

Fern Tims was a good friend, and I took care of her beauty needs for over 30 years. She often made 2 loaves of Zucchini Bread – one for me and one for her. This recipe yields 2 loaves.

## ZUCCHINI BREAD
in memory of Fern Tims

3 eggs
1 cup oil
2 cups sugar
2 cups peeled zucchini squash (grated or chopped real fine)
3 tsp. vanilla
3⅓ cups flour
1 tsp. salt
½ tsp. soda
1 tsp. baking powder
1 tsp. cinnamon
½ tsp. ginger and cloves

Beat eggs and add to sugar and oil. Add zucchini and vanilla. Sift dry ingredients together. Place in well-greased loaf pans. Bake 1 hour at 350° until done.

## CARROT BREAD

3 eggs (well-beaten)
½ cup cooking oil
2½ cups flour (sifted)
1 cup sugar
1 tsp. cinnamon
1⅓ cup coconut

**KITCHEN KAPERS:** If you are 1 egg short for a recipe, substitute 1 tsp. of cornstarch and add 3-4 Tbsp. of liquid.

½ cup raisins
½ cup pecans (chopped)
½ tsp. salt
½ cup milk
1 tsp. baking powder
1 tsp. baking soda
2 cups grated carrots
(shredded)
½ cup maraschino cherries
(snipped)

In a large bowl mix flour, sugar, baking powder, baking soda, cinnamon, and salt. Add egg mixture and mix enough just to combine. Stir in rest of the ingredients. Bake at 350° for about 50 - 55 minutes.

My grandmother would make egg butter when she came to visit us every summer.

## EGG BUTTER
in memory of Ollie Rogers
circa 1910

Bring 1 pint of sorghum molasses to a boil. Have ready two beaten eggs. Add allspice and cinnamon and stir in eggs and continue stirring until it thickens which will be as soon as it boils up. My grandmother would add ½ cup water to take away the rich taste. This makes a good spread for hot biscuits with butter.

# ALL BRAN MUFFINS
very nice to serve for brunch

2 Tbsp. shortening
¼ cup sugar
1 egg
1 cup all bran
¼ cup milk
1 cup flour
¼ tsp. salt
2½ tsp. baking powder

Cream shortening with sugar. Add egg and beat well. Soak all bran in milk until most of the moisture is absorbed. Stir only until the flour disappears – about 20 strokes. Fill greased muffin tins about ¾ full of batter. Bake about 30 minutes in 400° oven. Yields about 8-12 large muffins.

To substitute sour milk or buttermilk for sweet milk, add ¼ tsp. soda and reduce baking powder to 1 tsp.

To make bacon muffins, add ½ cup of crisped minced bacon to dry ingredients.

nut muffins: add ½ cup nuts.

orange muffins: add 2 Tbsp. grated orange rind being careful not to use any of the white part of rind next to the orange sections.

prune muffins: add ½ cup chopped prunes that have been soaked and drained. Cut in small pieces.

spice muffins: add 1 Tbsp. molasses and ½ tsp. ginger or 1 tsp. cinnamon.

## AUNT SUE'S BLUEBERRY MUFFINS

2 cups flour
3 Tbsp. sugar
3 tsp. baking powder
¼ tsp. salt
3 Tbsp. shortening (melted)
½ cup milk
½ cup blueberries
        (well-drained)
1 egg (well-beaten)

Sift flour and measure. Mix with flour, baking powder, salt and sugar. Add blueberries, shortening and milk. Mix only until blended. Fill well-oiled muffin tins ⅔ full. Bake in 400° oven for 12 - 15 minutes. Yields about 12 servings.

It's better to have loved and lost than to have never loved at all.

This is another handwritten recipe that was in Aunt Sue's 1927 P.T.A. cookbook. Anytime the recipe calls for sweet milk you know it's an old recipe.

## APRICOT UPSIDE DOWN MUFFINS
### in memory of Aunt Sue

Sift together 2 cups flour, ½ cup sugar, 3 Tbsp. baking powder, ½ tsp. salt, and add ¼ cup sweet milk. Beat until batter is smooth and light. Place 1 tsp. butter and 1 tsp. of brown sugar in each muffin tin. Heat until melted and well- blended. Put in a cooked dried apricot half. Cut petal shape in 3 sections in each pan. Cut side up. Fill pans half full of batter and bake in a slow oven until well done. Turn on to plate upside down. Use any king of dried fruit desired.

This recipe is Evie Clinkscales, a long time resident of Jackson County, Oklahoma, and daughter-in-law of Pearl Sloan and mother of Helen Sloan Peyton. Look for more of her recipes in the book.

## ALL BRAN ROLLS

1 cup fat or shortening
¾ cup flour
1 cup Kellogg All Bran
1½ tsp. salt
6½ cups flour or more
1 cup boiling water
2 eggs

2 cakes Fleischman's yeast
1 cup warm water

Put fat, sugar, all bran, and salt in mixing bowl, add boiling water. Stir until
melted. Put yeast in warm water.
Beat eggs separately. Add egg yolks
to above mixture. Put in half of flour.
Fold in egg whites beaten stiff. Then
add other flour. Put in covered bowl.
Let stay in icebox. Use as needed.
Bake at 425° for 15 minutes.

This is an old recipe and was used for a bread substitute. It was considered a treat when served with jelly or jam. Jellies and jams were a treat at our house. Sugar was considered very expensive. We only had jellies when we had company. There was always sorghum or Mary Jane or Karo Syrup.

## EGG CAKE
circa 1906

5 eggs (well beaten)
1 cup flour
1 tsp. baking powder
1 cup sweet milk

Beat the eggs well. Blend baking
powder in flour and add alternately
to milk. Pour into skillet containing
several Tbsp. of hot oil. Fry until cakes
begin to brown. Cut and turn each
piece. Fry until done. Serve hot with
butter and jelly.

Nothing will improve a man's hearing more than praise.

The pioneer mothers worked hard to furnish us with wholesome food without knowing how wonderful it was. The fresh vegetables, the homemade breads, sorghum molasses, and eggs that were so rich in iron furnished us with wholesome food and lots of energy.

## HOMINY GRIT SPOON BREAD

2 cups milk
1 scant cup hominy grits
3 egg yolks (well beaten)
egg whites
1 tsp. baking powder
1 tbsp. butter

Heat the milk to scalding. Stir in salt and grits. Add butter. Remove from fire and cool slightly. Stir in egg yolks. Beat the egg whites until stiff with the baking powder. Fold in buttered baking dish. Bake about 40 minutes at 350°. Now we would probably add grated cheese to the top. This bread would be considered very nutritious.

# SALADS
## AND
## SOUPS

All kinds of pickles were canned, and we used them mostly in potato salad. We never heard of hamburgers. I remember my very first hamburger. We were moving from Texas to Oklahoma. We had started early and had reached Electra, Texas, by noon. My father went in a cafe and bought us hamburgers, and we ate them in the car – no "drive-thru." How good they were!

Potato salad went to "dinner on the ground," when we had a Revival once every Summer. We always had lots of fried chicken that was fried in equal parts of lard and butter; nothing is better for frying chicken. There were always beet pickles and deviled eggs made with dry mustard, vinegar and a pinch of sugar. Desserts were usually fruit cobblers or cakes. The dinner had to be prepared while fixing breakfast. The breakfast wasn't dry cereal either; it cost too much and wouldn't "stick to the ribs." Breakfast consisted of Mothers Oats that had to be cooked for 20 minutes. Then there was sausage, fried ham or home cured salt pork (bacon). The bacon was too salty, cut too thick and too fat. We soaked it in sweet milk to take out part of the salt. We sharpened the knife on the rock door step in order to slice the salt pork thinner. It was still too salty, sliced too thin and was too fat. But it was still too salty, too thick and too fat. We also had scrambled eggs and usually had cream gravy made from the ham, sausage or bacon drippings. And of course, there were those big fluffy buttermilk biscuits made with lard, and a big bowl of freshly churned butter on the table. The biscuits were served with homemade sorghum or Mary Jane Corn Syrup. Jelly was only for company; sugar cost too much.

I grew up on all that "stuff" that's a no-no now. I still eat it in moderation. Would you believe that I'm still living at 83 and hale and hearty? It didn't matter what we ate or how much; we worked it off.

# OLD TIMEY POTATO SALAD
from past days

3-4 medium potatoes
6 Tbsp. vinegar
½ cup chopped sweet or sour
    pickles (home canned)
½ cup onion (chopped)
½ cup celery (diced)
    Now we can use fresh instead of
    the seeds.
⅓ cup sugar
¾ cup of salad dressing
    Then we used enough butter to give
    it a buttered seasoned taste.
3 hard cooked eggs
2 Tbsp. butter
salt and pepper to taste

Boil potatoes and cook until barely tender. Drain. Add butter (while hot), if not using salad dressing. Next add sugar, pepper, salt, and vinegar. Mash and add onion, pickles, eggs, and salad dressing. Now, I add ¼ cup or more of chopped celery. It wasn't available in the early days. My mother saved some of the yolks and grated to decorate the top. Put in serving bowl. I just love the combination of the sugar and vinegar without the salad dressing. That's the way everybody did it. I never saw the potatoes diced until after World War II. If diced, it needs to set overnight.

# TIPS ON TOSSED GREEN SALAD
## WITH FRENCH DRESSING

To start with, let's use the right salad bowl. It should never be used for anything else and washed by itself by only scalding. When dried, wrap it in waxed paper and put on a shelf by itself. We have so many kitchen gadgets now. I hope you can find a place just for the wooden bowl, ready for the next salad making. Use wooden spoon and fork. Rub the bowl with a split garlic clove.

Use the freshest crisp vegetables possible. Lettuce should never be cut, just torn apart. Tomatoes peeled and cut in wedges. Onions cut in thin crisp circles, better still if fresh green young onions in season. Celery should be crisp. When vegetables are ready, shake the French Dressing, toss lightly with the dressing, making sure each particle is coated with a thin layer of dressing. You can vary this recipe to create your own salad. Always serve on a chilled plate or bowl. There's nothing worse than a limp green salad.

This is just as good as you'll find in the grocery store.

## AUNT LELA'S
## PREPARED MUSTARD

3 tsp. ground mustard
½ cup vinegar
1 Tbsp. sugar
a dash of salt
2 egg yolks (beaten)
lump of butter (size of an egg)

Put the ground mustard in a bowl and add warm water to make a paste. Blend until smooth. Add vinegar, sugar, beaten eggs, salt, and put the butter in last. Cook in heavy small saucepan until thickens.

## CHICKEN SALAD

Skin and bone chicken breasts the amount needed. Boil until tender. Let cool and run through a food processor. Mix with your favorite dressing. I use mayonnaise and a little mustard, enough to spread easily. Stir in the amount of red or green grapes (seedless), as you desire. Use as a sandwich spread on grain bread or English muffins. Very filling on hamburger buns, if you use quite a bit of spread. The chicken will keep in the refrigerator several days.

# AUNT SUE'S
# WINTER WALDORF SALAD
circa 1955

2 large delicious apples
½ cup midget marshmallows
½ cup cubed celery
¼ cup nuts (chopped)
1 tsp. lemon juice
½ cup mayonnaise
1 Tbsp. thick cream
1 Tbsp. cherry juice

Cube apples without peeling, sprinkle with lemon juice. Add marshmallows, celery and nuts. Mix well. Thin mayonnaise with cream and cherry juice. Add to other ingredients, tossing lightly. Serve on lettuce leaf. For decorative effect, add rings of thinly sliced apples.

A treat you can make ahead of time for those hot Summer days.

# TUNA SALAD

1 can (9 oz.) chunk tuna
1 cup celery (chopped)
2 Tbsp. sweet pickle juice
½ cup Spring onions with
        green tops (finely chopped)
½ cup mayonnaise
1 Tbsp. mustard (prepared)
3 hard boiled eggs (chopped)
½ cup sweet pickles (chopped)

Cook and drain 7 oz. package of salad noodles. Let cool. Stir in with rest of ingredients that have been mixed in a large bowl. Serve on lettuce leaf and sprinkle with paprika.

## CABBAGE CHRISTMAS SALAD
in memory of Fern Tims

½ cup sugar
1 Tbsp. flour
1 Tbsp. corn flour
½ tsp. cornstarch
½ tsp. salt
⅓ tsp. pepper
⅓ tsp. dry mustard
1 can (8½ oz.) pineapple tidbits
water
¾ cups white vinegar
2 eggs (beaten)
6 cups cabbage (shredded)
1 cup miniature marshmallows
1 unpeeled red apple (cored and cut into wedges)
pecan halves

Combine first 6 ingredients in saucepan. Drain pineapple and add enough water to make 1½ cup juice. Stir juice and vinegar into dry ingredients. Beat in eggs. Cook over medium heat until it thickens, stirring constantly. Cool well. Toss with cabbage, marshmallows, pineapple, and apple. Garnish with pecans.

# OLIVE AND EGG SALAD

3 hard cooked eggs
   (chopped)
4 Tbsp. olives (chopped)

Mix eggs and olives with enough cooked salad dressing to moisten well.

Cooked salad dressing:
2 eggs
5 Tbsp. sugar
½ tsp. salt
3 Tbsp. flour
paprika
1 tsp. prepared mustard
½ vinegar
1 cup Pet milk

Beat egg yolks well. Add sugar, salt, paprika, mustard, and flour. Heat vinegar to boiling. Pour over egg mixture, beating constantly. Add milk gradually and cook into heavy saucepan. Cook until thickens. Cool. Makes 2 cups.

## AVOCADO SALAD
Olevia Robinson

1 pkg. lime Jell-O
2 cups hot water
1 avocado (mashed)
1 pkg. (3 oz.) cream cheese
½ cup mayonnaise
½ cup celery (chopped)

1 green pepper (chopped)
1 tsp. onion juice
a dash of salt
small amount of pimento

Dissolve Jell-O in hot water and set aside to cool. Cream cheese and mix together with mayonnaise and avocado. Stir in celery, green pepper, onion juice, and salt. Add this to mixture of Jell-O when it begins to set. Garnish with pimento. Serves 8-12.

## CREAM FRUIT SALAD
Jeannette Weaver

½ cup sugar
2 eggs
½ tsp. salt
2 tsp. flour juice from 1 can of
    pineapple
1 large can pineapple chunks
2 oranges (peel and dice)
24 marshmallows
1 cup pecans 1 pint whipped
    cream

Cream sugar, eggs, salt, flour, and pineapple juice. Cook until thickened. Take off stove. Cool. Add oranges, pineapple, pecans, and marshmallows. Whip cream and add or fold it into fruit mix. Refrigerate and serve cold.

# FROZEN SURPRISE SALAD
Sue Parker
Springfield, TN
modern

1 medium container of Cool Whip
1 can (10 oz.) frozen strawberries (thawed)
1 no. 2 can pineapple (drained)
3 bananas
1 cup pecans (chopped)

Mix Cool Whip, strawberries and pineapple in large bowl. Fold bananas and ¾ cup of pecans in mixture. Pour mixture in large pan and freeze Cut frozen salad in 1½" squares. Place squares on small plate, topped with whip cream. Garnish with fresh mint sprigs. So refreshing in hot weather.

# STRAWBERRY AND CREAM
Olevia Robinson

1 large pkg. strawberry Jell-O
2 cup boiling water
2 pkgs. (10 oz.) frozen strawberries (or 1 large pkg.)
1½ cup pineapple (crushed)
1 cup sour cream
whole strawberries for garnish

Dissolve Jell-O in water, add strawberries and stir until thawed. Add pineapple and pour half the mixture into 8"x8" dish. Chill until firm. Spread sour cream over Jell-O mixture in an even layer. Pour remaining Jell-O over sour cream. Chill until firm. Cut in squares and garnish with sour cream and whole strawberries. Serves 10.

## CORN CHOWDER

1 can corn
1 pint water
½ cup butter
2 Tbsp. onion (chopped)
¼ cup flour
2 tsp. salt
¼ tsp. pepper
1 quart milk
2 egg yolks (beaten)

Cook corn with 1 pint water. Let come to a boil. Reduce to a simmer. Cook onion in butter until a light brown. Add flour and seasoning and milk gradually. Pour soup slowly over beaten eggs. If you want it thicker, add some instant potatoes.

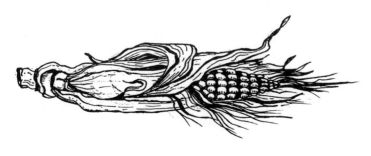

# THREE WEEK SLAW

1 large head of cabbage
       (grated or chopped,
       blender works well)
1 large onion (chopped)
1 large bell pepper (chopped)

Dressing for cabbage:
1 cup vinegar
2 Tbsp. sugar
1 Tbsp. salt
1 cup sugar
1 tsp. celery seed
1 tsp. dry mustard
¾ cup salad oil

Put cabbage in large bowl. Place onion and green pepper on top; do not stir. Sprinkle 2 Tbsp. of sugar over all. Do not stir. Now for the dressing. Put into saucepan, vinegar, sugar, salt, celery, and mustard. Bring to boil, remove from heat, and add oil. Pour over cabbage mixture. Do not Stir. Cover and put in refrigerator for 4-5 hours. Now it's time to stir and mix well. Put into covered containers; 1 big Tupperware will work. Keep refrigerated. Will keep for 3 weeks if you horde it. It's a good carry-out dish.

I have cooked this stew on national television, including QVC – the cable television shopping network. The feedback on this recipe has been tremendous.

## CABBAGE PATCH STEW

Make 1 lb. pork sausage in walnut size balls and steam with enough water to barely cover. Cook while preparing next 3 ingredients. Add 1 cup onions (diced), 1 cup celery (diced) and ½ cup bell peppers. Let steam for about 10 minutes and add 1 can whole kernel corn. Add 2 cups grated cabbage and 1 can tomatoes with juice. If I use whole tomatoes, I chop in can. Add salt and chili powder to taste. I cook it down fairly low. But if you want it thin, add more water. Great with corn bread.

## MARIE MILLS' CHICKEN SOUP

Boil 1 large broiler chicken until tender with plenty of water for broth. Cool and debone. Chicken chunks are preferred. Cook together in chicken broth ½ cup of rice (uncooked), 3-4 grated carrots, 1 large onion (diced), and 3-4 stalks of chopped celery. Cook until nearly tender. Then add chopped chicken and simmer for about 30 minutes. Add 2 packages of Lipton's Cup of Soup (optional). Salt and pepper to taste.

# MARVIN ALLEN'S STEW

1½-2 lbs. lean ground beef

Saute´ beef in heavy skillet until pink color is barely gone. In the mean-time, cook in a large pot until nearly done these ingredients (use plenty of water):

5 potatoes
1 large onion
4-6 carrots (sliced)
4-6 stalks celery (diced)
1 can tomatoes

Add meat, 3-4 dashes of Tabasco sauce, 4 tsp. Worcestershire sauce, salt and pepper to taste, and chili powder, if desired. Simmer for about 30 minutes. If thinner than you like, thicken with ½ cup rice (raw) and cook a little longer or thicken with instant potatoes. Paprika gives it a nice color. Serve with fresh corn bread.

# RELISHES

## AND

## PRESERVES

# AUNT SUE'S
# CANTALOUPE PICKLES

Select under-ripe cantaloupes. Cut into sections and remove rind. Soak in salt solution (4 Tbsp. salt to 1 quart of water) for 3 hours. Drain of brine and add the well-drained rind to a pickling syrup made from the following ingredients:

4 cups water
4 cups sugar
1 cup vinegar
1 Tbsp. cinnamon
1 Tbsp. allspice
1 Tbsp. cloves

Boil the rind rapidly for 10 minutes. Let stand overnight. Drain the syrup from cantaloupe and boil until it coats a spoon. Add cantaloupe and cook until clear about 1 hour. Seal immediately in clean hot jars.

A jar of these pickles was given to me by one of my clients in the middle '30s. These pickles are very crisp and good. This recipe was handwritten in Aunt Sue's P. T. A. cookbook.

## FOURTEEN DAY PICKLES

Slice, wash and cut in ¾" blocks enough for 2 gallons of pickles. Place in stone jars and pour over them 2 cups salt (canning salt), 1 gallon of boiling water; let stand 7 days. Skim everyday, if necessary. On 8th day, drain well and pour over them 1 gallon of boiling water. Let stand 24 hours. On 9th day, drain off and pour over them 1 gallon of boiling water and 1 Tbsp. of powdered alum. Let stand 24 hours. On 10th day, drain and pour over them 1 gallon of boiling water. Let stand 24 hours. On 11th day, drain well and place in clean jars. Pour over them, boiling hot the following syrup:

5 pints vinegar
6 cups sugar (part brown)
½ oz. celery seed
1 oz. stick of cinnamon

On 12th day, drain off syrup and add 1 cup of sugar. Let heat to boiling point and pour back over pickles. On 13th day, repeat 12th day instructions. On 14th day, seal. The cucumbers are never put in the boiling water. Just let stand in the liquid. That will make them soft.

This recipe was written on the back of Fern Tims F. T. D. scratch pad. Fern owned Altus Floral Company for many years.

# KOSHER DILLS
in memory of Fern Tims

20-25 medium size cucumbers
⅛ tsp. alum
1 grape leaf
1 clove of garlic
2 heads of dill
1 hot red pepper

Liquid solution:
1 quart vinegar
1 cup salt
3 quarts water

Wash cukes good. Let stand in water overnight. Pack in sterilized jars next day. Add alum, garlic, dill, red pepper, and grape leaf. Heat solution of vinegar, salt and water to boiling and pour into jars and seal. Let stand 6-8 weeks in dark cool place undisturbed. These will color milky-like, but eventually will clear. They may spew over the jars a little bit; it won't hurt.

# PLAIN SOUR PICKLES

Wash and place cucumbers in jars. Use 1 tsp. salt, 1 tsp. sugar to each 1 quart of vinegar. Heat just to bubbling stage. Pour over cucumbers and seal.

# DILL PICKLES

Select fresh nice size cucumbers. Wash and put into jars. Place several sprays of dill weed on top of cucumbers. Heat 1 quart of water and 1 quart of vinegar and ¼ cup of salt to boiling. Cool and pour over cucumbers, filling jars to ¼" of top. Seal, liquid will be cloudy in a few days, but will soon clear.

## SWEET PICKLES
in memory of Nellie Wilders
Hereford, Texas
a cousin of my father and Aunt Sue

Wash and put cucumbers on stove in cold salt water. Place in jars. Make syrup of 2 cups of vinegar, 1 cup water and 1 cup of sugar. Place in jars. Add spices as desired. Boil and pour over cucumbers and seal while hot.

# CRYSTAL PICKLES

Slice the cheapest large sour pickles in very thin slices. Place in a jar or large mixing bowl. Add an equal weight of sugar. Let stand for 3 days. The pickles will become clear and crisp and half the cost. This is a good trick to know.

# PEACH SWEET PICKLES

6 lbs. of fruit
3 lbs. of sugar
1 pint of vinegar

Peel and put in sugar and vinegar. Let boil until fruit is clear and tender. The syrup should be fairly thick; not real thick, and not watery thin. Put ground spices in bag and put in top of jar. Seal hot. The peaches should be cling. The little red Indian Peach is preferable.

## BEET PICKLES
### the modern way

1 can beets
½ tsp. salt
½ tsp. dry mustard
¼ cup beet liquor
½ clove of garlic
1 Tbsp. sugar
6 Tbsp. vinegar

Drain beets, combine mustard, sugar, salt, and cloves of garlic. Heat vinegar, beet liquor to boiling. Slowly add to the sugar mixture. Stir to blend well. Pour over beets when the mixture is smooth. Let set 4 hours before serving. Remove garlic. Especially good served with meats or fish.

This recipe came from the Ball Fruit Jar Company's Ball Blue Book, copyrighted in 1938.

## PICKLED WALNUTS

Pick young walnuts while they are soft enough to pierce with a needle. Soak them in a strong brine for 3 days, drain them and place in a stone crock. To a gallon of vinegar, add a cupful of sugar, 2 Tbsp. each of whole peppers and cloves, 1 Tbsp. allspice, and light blades of mace. Boil the mixture for 10 minutes. Pour the mixture over the walnuts while scalding hot and let stand for 3 days. Then drain off the vinegar mixture. Put the nuts into jars. Bring the vinegar to a boil. Pour over the nuts, seal and store in a cool place. They must season for at least 6 weeks before they are ready to serve.

# SQUASH PICKLES

Stella Robertson
Ticksfaw, LA

3 cups small yellow squash
(sliced)
3 cups sugar
2 cups white vinegar
2 tsp. mustard seed
2 tsp. celery seed
2 cups green peppers
(coarsely chopped)
2 cups sweet red peppers
(coarsely chopped)
2 large onions (sliced and
separated into rings)

Cover squash with salted water and let stand for 1 hour; drain. Combine sugar, vinegar, mustard, and celery seed in a large saucepan; bring to boiling and add squash, peppers and onion. Return to boiling and cook 5 minutes. Pack mixture in hot sterilized jars and seal. Process in boiling water bath for 10 minutes. Yields about 4 pints.

This is another squash pickle recipe from Molly Williams. Thanks, Molly, for this recipe. Somehow, I lost your address. Sorry about that. They are so good!

## MOLLY'S SQUASH PICKLES
Molly Williams

8 cups yellow squash (sliced paper thin)
2 cups onions (sliced paper thin)
1 cup chopped red sweet peppers ( canned pimentos)
or 2 cups green sweet peppers
2 Tbsp. canning salt
2 cups white vinegar
2 Tbsp. celery seed
2 Tbsp. mustard seed
3 cups water
⅛ tsp. alum

Spoon salt over squash and ice over squash and let set at least an hour. Add remaining ingredients and bring to a rolling boil. Boil 2-5 minutes. Seal in sterilized jars.

This recipe is different, delicious and a good meat accompaniment.

## ORANGE SWEET PICKLES

4 oranges
1 tsp. cinnamon
1 tsp. cloves
1½ cups vinegar
2 cups sugar

Peel oranges, remove all membrane. Cut into thick slices and steam until tender, Boil sugar, vinegar and spices tied into cheese cloth or soft piece of cloth like an old sheet for 25 minutes. Add fruit and simmer slowly for 1 hour. Place in jelly jars and let ripen.

## HOW TO PRESERVE A HUSBAND
from the Ball Glass Co. Blue Book

Be careful in your selection. Do not choose too young. When selected, give your entire thoughts to preparation for domestic use. Some wives insist upon keeping them in a pickle, others are constantly getting them into hot water. This may make them sour, hard, and sometimes bitter; even poor varieties may be made sweet, tender and good, by garnishing them with patience, well sweetened with love and seasoned with kisses. Wrap them in a mantle of charity. Keep warm with a steady fire of domestic devotion and serve with peaches and cream. Thus prepared, they will keep for years.

# CUCUMBER CINNAMON RINGS

Liz Hume
Tulsa, OK

2 gallon large cucumber rings
2 cups lime
3 cups vinegar
1 small bottle red food coloring
1 Tbsp. alum
10 cups sugar
8 sticks cinnamon bark
I large pkg. (8 oz.) or 2 small
    pkgs. red hots (candy)

Peel 2 gallons of large cucumber rings. Slice cucumbers ½" thick and core. Add 2 cups lime to 8½ quarts of water or enough water to cover cucumbers with the lime mixed in and let stand 24 hours. Drain and wash. Soak rings in cold water for 3 hours. Drain. Simmer them in 1 cup vinegar, 1 small bottle of red food coloring, 1 Tbsp. of alum, and enough water to cover. Simmer for 2 hours. Drain. Make syrup of 2 cups vinegar, 2 cups water, 10 cups sugar, 8 sticks cinnamon bark, and red hots. Bring to a boil. Pour over rings and let stand overnight. Drain. Save syrup and reheat syrup. Repeat this step for 3 days. Third day pack rings in jars. Put reheated syrup over pickle rings. Seal jars. Put jars in a boiling water bath for 10 minutes to seal jars.

I can still see Aunt Lela's big dishpan of peeled pears, ready for making preserves.

Peel and cut into eights as many pears as desired. They will cook down about half of what you started with. To 2 lbs. of pears, Aunt Lela would add 4 cups of sugar. Let set overnight. It make its own liquid. Heat through real well. Lower heat. She cooked in oven. Most people cook it until clear and tender. Aunt Lela cooked the hard pears "kinda" like candy and were tough. So good on hot biscuits.

## PUMPKIN PRESERVES

5 pints of pumpkin
8 cups sugar
3 lemons
1 tsp. salt

Cut pumpkins into slices ¼" thick and 1-2" long. Place in earthen bowl or preserving kettle. Add the sugar and let stand overnight. Drain and boil the liquid until it threads. Add the pumpkin, thinly sliced lemons and salt. Cook mixture until it is thick and clear. Seal while hot in clean hot jars.

# STRAWBERRY PRESERVES

1 quart fresh and ripe straw-
     berries (crushed)
1 box Sure-Jell
¾ cup water
4 cups granulated sugar
6 – ½ pint jars

Wash and scald jars and lids. Drain good. Measure crushed strawberries, 1 layer at a time, alternating with sugar. Mix well. Combine ¾ cup water and Sure-Jell in saucepan and bring to a boil. Boil for 1 minute, stirring constantly. Stir into fruit mixture. Continue to stir for 3 minutes. A few crystals may remain. Quickly ladle into jars. Cover for 24 hours and store in refrigerator.

**This preserve stand has been in the family as long as I can remember.**

photograph by Michael Allen

217

## AUNT LELA'S PEACH PRESERVES
my favorite

1 lb. peaches
1 cup water
1½ cups sugar

Make a syrup of sugar and water by heating just until sugar is dissolved. Let cool at room temperature. Pour over peaches and allow to stand overnight. Next morning cook until fruit is clear. Remove peaches and cook syrup until thick. Add the peaches to syrup. Heat and seal.

## ORANGE MARMALADE

6 oranges
1 lemon

Peel and cut into small pieces the amount you want. The proportion: 6 part orange to 1 part lemon. Cut the peel into very fine strips, removing the membrane. To each pound of fruit, put 3 pints of water. Soak for 24 hours. Then boil until tender, set aside until next day. To 1 pint of boiled fruit, add 1½ pounds of sugar. Boil until the fruit is transparent and the syrup jells. It will be a golden color, if cooked in shallow pan.

# STRAWBERRY SUN PRESERVES

Most people think that strawberry juice is thickened by the sun is the best. The flavor seems to be more like fresh strawberries, and the color is very good. Wash, stem and weigh ripe berries. Use about ⅔ of the firmest and largest berries whole and save the smaller ⅓ for making juice. Prepare the juice by crushing the berries. A lb. of berries will make a lb. of juice. Use 1 lb. of sugar to ½ cup juice. Cook the juice for 3 minutes and strain. Add the sugar to the strained juice and heat slowly until sugar is dissolved. Then remove from heat. Drop the selected fruit in the hot syrup, let stand for a minute. Place on a shallow pan. Don't let the berries touch. Boil the remaining syrup for about 10 minutes. Pour this over the berries. One tbsp. lemon juice can be added to syrup. Cover pan with window glass to protect from dusk and set in sun. Leave out for 3 consecutive days. Bring in before dew falls.

# What Can I Give?

I think of the things God has given me
  and I know that the gifts were full and free,
He sent His Son from His home above
  Have I returned that matchless love?

Do I care enough that He made it all
  from the canyon deep...to the mountain tall.
He made the sun...and the rolling sea,
  He did it all as a gift for me.

What have I done to express to Him,
  as I stand in awe on the canyon's rim,
"Thank you Lord," for letting me live.
  And for all the things I have to give!

I have this day...and my talents, too,
  but all that I have belongs to You.
So...what can I give from my life's stocked shelf,
  I'll give it...I'll give myself!

Ed Lobaugh

Ed Lobaugh is the minister of Elm and Hudson Church of Christ, Altus, Oklahoma, where I have attended for over 60 years.

# MEMORIES

Photograph by Michael Allen
setting in the home of Thelma Allen

# So Much To Do

There was so much that the pioneer women had to do, like sewing, mending and darning. My mother made all our clothes except coats and sweaters; they were "store bought." Most of the mens clothing were bought except for work shirts and underwear. I remember my mother had a blue serge suit that was worn with a waist as it was called then.

There was the wash day, ironing day and probably the hardest was the hog killing days. On the hog killing days, there was lard to render, sausage to make and sack, soap to be made in the big black iron kettle. The mincemeat was to made from the hog's head which was important to our school dinner. Some pickled the hog's feet, but we never did. They were cooked with the hog's head and made into mincemeat. This was done in the Winter months.

In the Spring there was the gardening and canning. What we didn't eat fresh, we canned for use in the Winter months.

We raised our own popcorn. It didn't pop like Orville Redenbacher's, but it still made good popcorn balls on snowy days when we couldn't go to school. Sometimes, it was too cold to ride in the buggy.

We left some of the beans and peas in the field to mature for use in the Winter. We gathered them in early Fall in a cotton picking sack or a gunney sack. They had to be winnowed. That means we beat them with a broom while still in the sack to break the dry shells. Then we held them up as high as we could. The wind would separate the dry shells from the dry peas or beans that would be stored in gallon syrup buckets. We wrapped some kind of powder in a little round cloth bag tied with twine string from the country store. This bag was placed in the top of a gallon bucket to keep the weevils out. Or was it to kill the eggs? I wish I knew. I don't remember what the powder was called. I'm sure I knew at the time; my "recaller" is not as good as it once was.

My father and brother, Charlie, milked the cows (we always

milked 2 or 3 cows), separated the milk from the cream and "slopped" the pigs. We girls had to churn and mold the butter. Churning was just about the most monotonous job anyone could do on the farm. We sold our surplus butter and cream.

There were little chickens to be raised. They were hatched in a small incubator in the cellar. That incubator was called "The Little Red Hen." Some folks raised turkeys to sell, and the market was good around Thanksgiving and Christmas. Now, we can enjoy turkey the year around. We never raised turkeys. It was too time consuming. The turkeys would wander too far away from home, sometimes as far as 2-3 miles, looking for grasshoppers and insects to eat. They would never come home, so someone had to bring them home to feed and water them before dark.

Women have always worked and help make the living. Then we did it for survival. Now it is done to buy what we would call luxuries back then. My father use to say, "God didn't promise us a rose garden."

photograph by Michael Allen

This is the Wesson Oil crock I told you about in my first cookbook. My daughter found the missing beater in an antique store.

# Snow Ice Cream

We couldn't make ice cream until nearly bedtime. That was a long time to wait for such a treat. Today, kids can have it when they come home from school. Then there were so many chores to do, like bringing in the wood from the woodpile to the front porch and putting it in the woodbox in the kitchen for the cookstove. There might not be enough wood cut, so my brother, Charlie, had to do that. We also checked the kindling that started the fires. My father always built the fires. First the ashes were removed from the stove, then crumpled paper was put down, then the kindling was placed over the paper and next were the chips that had to be brought in from the woodpile. The stove wood was put on the very top last. Then it was time to light the paper with a match. Coal oil was never used – too dangerous. The kindling was made from pine boxes that came from the store. Just about everything came in those wood boxes. They have long since been replaced by brown paper bags and pasteboard boxes. The shavings were made from these boxes with my father's pocket knife. Then, every man, young and old, had a knife in his pocket, very essential but hard on pockets. I've seen my mother mend "many a pocket." She just replaced them with new ones that she had made, unbelievable now. It's hard to realize that there was a time in the past, when wood was so essential.

We had to check the lamps to make sure there was enough oil to last through those long winter nights. For us they were not that long. We went to bed early and got up early. There had to be enough oil to last until bedtime. In the winter it was dark when we got up, so there had to be enough to last until daylight the next morning.

If the water froze for the chickens, it had to be replaced with warm water. The eggs had to be gathered to keep from freezing if left in the chicken house. In the summer the snakes would get them. They were so essential for our livelihood.

The water level in the well would do down in the night,

so we had to see that there was a big pitcher of water brought into the house to prime the pump. If not brought in, it would be frozen solid by morning. Many times it would be icy in the house. To bring the water level up the next morning, we poured the water in the pump and pumped as fast as we could. It worked! Now you know why the water bucket and teakettle were full of water when we went to bed.

By the time the cows were milked and the cream separated by our father and brother, my mother had the supper on the table. Then there were the dishes to do. Our father saw that our mother sat down in our only rocker while Marie and I washed the dishes and all those old milk vessels. I've never even mentioned the churning of the butter. While our mother was resting in that rocker, she usually had something to do in her lap, such as mending, darning socks or just crocheting for fun. There was no radio, television, cassette tape recorder or telephone to call our girl friends, just the Dallas Semi-Weekly newspaper that was brought to us by the rural mail carrier. We couldn't hear what the President or Congress had done that day, but maybe that was good. Girls didn't call boys in those days; the boys were expected to do the calling.

We knew there would be no ice cream until we got "our lessons," so we got busy with that; maybe we slighted it some. When we got everything done, we lit the lantern that set by the front door, grabbed the biggest dishpan and made a "high dive" for the outdoors. We filled it "brimming full" with snow. It had to be the second snow; the first snow had germs from the air, and we never heard of pollution. We left the snow in the pan and put in sugar and vanilla to taste, and then we added rich milk until it was of the right consistency. We ate until we were "full as a tick" and "cold as a frog." After eating the ice cream, we grabbed that hot rock wrapped in part of an old quilt, jumped into bed and covered up "head and ears." We were then snug as a "bug in a rug" and drifted off to slumberland as "happy as a lark."

# My Brother Charlie

When we were on the farm, we had one hundred acres of the most beautiful grassland, but there was no market for cattle. Now all that has changed; all that land is owned by prosperous ranchers. I recall after we left the farm in Texas and moved to a very small town in Oklahoma, we had a milk cow in town. Can you believe that? This cow had twin calves, and at that time had no value. They had to be weaned from the cow, because we needed the milk for family consumption. We couldn't feed them, so we had to give them away to a man who furnished beef to the surrounding grocers. He had to feed them for a year or more before he could market them.

One of the saddest times was when I was in my middle teens in The Depression. Everybody was affected by The Depression; some worse than others. Some of my father's cousins, Jess and Nellie Wilders, sent word to us that they could use my brother's help on their farm near Hereford, Texas. My brother, Charlie, was here in Oklahoma 150 miles away and literally had no money to get there. He left the next day, hitchhiking. It was sad to see him go, but really sad when we didn't know when he would get there. What if he didn't get there by night? Where would he sleep? What would he do for something to eat? We wouldn't know for several days. We had no phone, and he had no money. Aunt Maude, who lived next door, came to the rescue. I remember she put a few coins in his hand, less than a dollar, and he was on his way. Luckily, Charlie got there in 4-5 hours and found a ride to the Wilders" home with one of their neighbors in just a few minutes after arriving in the area. In the meantime we didn't know whether he got there or not. He left with a penny postcard in his pocket for the purpose of letting us know to his "where-abouts." This was in the Spring, and he rode the train at Thanksgiving to see us. I know it was Thanksgiving, because Marie and I took advantage of being out of school to pick cotton. Charlie went with us to the cotton field to help us and also catch the train back to Hereford. While waiting for the train to come by, he picked cotton, taking turns to put it in both of our sacks. Then when he heard the train coming just about three or four blocks away, he got on the track and hailed it down. We missed him and hated to see him go, but we were glad he had a good place to live. The Wilders loved him and was treated like a son. They had five children, none grown. Charlie loved the children, and they loved him. He lived with Jess and Nellie until my father traded a cow for a truck, creating work for both of them. Twelve years before his death, Charlie went into commercial combining of wheat; a trade he learned from the Wilders.

I still miss Charlie. He and his wife, Christine, were living next door to me when he died at the age of 59 of cancer. My sister-in-law has long since died. He had a sense of humor which I'm sure helped him and all of us through those trying times.

**Charlie and Christine Rogers**
photograph by Marvin Allen

# Entertainment

We did a lot of things for entertainment. We made our own dolls from corncobs dressed with scraps our mother gave us. We also used medicine bottles, even though we didn't have a lot of medicine, just cough syrup and Baby Percy. We would take a round piece of cloth and put cotton in it to make the head and stick it down into the medicine bottle. We would dress them, too.

My mother would make us a checkerboard out of black and red buttons and colored the squares on pasteboard. The boys played marbles. We even rode calves before that got too big and rode the old sows; they were not very dangerous. Then there were picnics we went to on the Fourth of July. My mother wasn't very crazy about those picnics, but she knew we had fun. We had lemonade in a tub, and we all went in the wagon, because the buggy wouldn't carry the whole family. We would take the endgate off the wagon and dangle our feet on the ground. That was lots of fun.

photograph by Michael Allen

# The Horse and The Sweater

There were about three families that went to school in buggies that tied the horses to the same tree. Every day from the beginning of school my mother would say, "You'd better take your sweater; it might come a 'northerner'." And sure enough, sometimes we would see that old blue northerner, coming across the country, black as it could be with tumbleweeds landing on the barbed wire fences. One day somebody's horse chewed up my sister's little red sweater, well just one cuff. It was a machine knitted sweater. So my mother found some contrasting thread, made a crocheted cuff on both sleeves, crocheted a little scallop edge on the collar and also crocheted some buttons to tie it all together. When she was finished, the sweater looked like it was styled that way. This was a good example of pioneer ingenuity.

# One Christmas

On Friday at school we got to go upstairs and usually one of teachers could play the piano, and we would sing old songs like "Old My Darling Nellie Gray," "Bring Back My Bonnie To Me," and "The Star-Spangled Banner." At Christmas time, we sang "Silent Night." We never had a Christmas tree at home, but we always had a community tree at school. The boys on the last day of school before Christmas vacation would go out and cut down a pine tree. The girls would string popcorn and make chains out of newspaper strips and glue them with flour and water paste. Those were our tree decorations. Our parents took our Christmas presents and hung them on the tree. Someone would play "Santa Claus" and pass out those toys. In 1926 we had no Christmas at all. My aunt who had six children was gravely ill with typhoid fever. The creek nearby the well ran over and contaminated the water and brought mosquitoes. She died on the first day of 1927. My parents went over to their house to help take care of the six children. We spent Christmas week with an aunt that took care of us. She tried to make it fun for us, but my folks didn't get to go to town to buy presents.

Usually we received two presents for Christmas: a doll and maybe my mother would make some doll clothes. But this Christmas we understood. The three younger children of the six lived with us until they got old enough for their daddy to bring them back home. It wasn't uncommon for us to cook a gallon of potatoes every day. We couldn't afford it, but we just moved over and made room for the kids. I suppose there were homes to take care of them, but most people took care of their own.

## We Saved Everything!

We found a use for everything. We needed no wastebaskets. If it wasn't reusable, it went into the heater or cookstove. Even the "Farm and Ranch," a monthly magazine, was made into coat hangers. The good part of my mother's skirts were made into cook aprons and sunbonnets. When the men's wool pants were no longer wearable, they were made into lap robes for the buggy and later on for the cars. The flour sacks were turned into tea towels or maybe kitchen curtains. Sometimes sugar or salt came in a cloth sack. They were smaller than the flour sacks, and they made dish rags. The best part of towels were made into wash cloths. Parts of the men's work shirts were torn into strips to make rag rugs that were especially good to step on before the house warmed up in the cold winter mornings. My mother would make our summer underwear out of the flour sacks. We never had "48#" written across the back. My mother took great pains to see that all the printing was off. It wouldn't have mattered if the printing was left on; nobody would have seen it anyway. We were always admonished when we sat down, " Put your dress down and don't cross your legs." Ladies, we were told, always carried a handkerchief. The best parts of sheets were made into squares of different sizes to use as lids on food products. Milk was put into large crocks; more cream rose to the top if stored in that manner. The cloth was wrapped around the container "Aunt Jemima Style."

The wash shelf was on the back porch in the Summer. It held the water bucket and dipper, wash pan and a saucer or bucket lid for a soap dish. It was usually Kirks Hard Water Soap or Lava for the mens' greasy hands from putting axle grease in the buggy or wagon wheels.

## Our Early Household

When Marvin and I married, he had rented a 2-bedroom house for $10⁰⁰ a month. We had a very inexpensive living room suit, breakfast table and 4 chairs, and a bedroom suit for the front bedroom. And there was a 9'x12' wool rug for the living room floor. We had no furniture for the back bedroom, so the grocer helped us out. He saved us two orange crates for a dressing table. We stood them on end about 2½ to 3 feet apart and went to the lumberyard and bought a 1"x12" board to connect these two boxes for a dressing table. Then it was draped with a floral skirt for no more than 15¢. Then while at the lumberyard, they gave us an empty nail keg that we padded and draped for a stool. Pretty neat, don't you think? I don't remember what we did for curtains, just cheap shades I presume. Venetian blinds came a decade or more later. The bed was just a cheap iron bed with springs and a mattress filled with cotton we had raised before we left the farm.

## The Beauty Shop

The beauty shops were so different from our fancy salons of today. The process of permanent waving was so uncomfortable. The heaters were pulled down from a central unit and heated with electricity and occasionally would burn a blister on your head. You blew on the heater with your mouth, funneled the air through a paper, or you might have a blower on the same principle as the handheld hair dryer, but with cold air.

The hair was blocked in spaces about 2½"-3" wide. Then each space of hair was pulled through a piece of felt that was slit through the middle. Then there was what we called a "spacer" that we put on top of the felt pad. It held a place that the roller fit into, called the rod and roller. Then the hair was put between the spacer and closed. The next step before wrapping was to cut the hair. Each section of hair that was in the spacer, you might say, was cut by guess. You had to be pretty good to get the desired length, not too long in length, not to short on top for a wave, or enough length to cover the ears. Then you saturated the hair in curling solution and wrapped the hair on the curler that fit in the spacer. The next step was to wet the same amount of pads for each roller, to go on just before the heaters. The solution softened the hair, so it would form a curl. It's the same principle with the cold wave, except the solution wrapped on the curler is done by a chemical and the neutralizer stops and sets the curl. The pad you put on before the heater was two pieces, one tinfoil about 2½"x3" with a piece of fleece sewn together, both pieces the same size, well saturated with solution. After you get the heaters turned on, you keep hoping you don't leave it on too long or take it off too soon. By then it began to get hot to the head, you start blowing and still hoping all your efforts will prevent a blister. This machine cost from $200$^{00}$ to $300$^{00}$. The solution came in a glass gallon jug, and you could buy it for $1$^{00}$. Labor was cheap during The Depression. Permanents were $1$^{00}$, if not on sale for 75¢.

I recall a friend of ours and her daughter drove to Oklahoma City, a distance of 150 miles one way for permanents. They didn't get finished, so they had to spend the night and go back the next morning to finish. The price of the first permanents were a dollar per curl, and there were about 25 curls. This was in the early twenties when beauty shops were scarce.

The water was so hard before the days of softeners, and there were no detergents. They came after World War II – a wonderful improvement. We made gallons of shampoo by filling the glass gallon jugs that our permanent solution came in with shavings from a bar of Kirks Hard Water Soap. The cost was 5¢ a gallon. With the water so hard, there was no sheen, and it would tangle. So the only remedy was a vinegar rinse. This was 10-15 years before cream rinse. We ordered vinegar by the 50 gallon barrel, wooden with staves around them, just like we use now for decorations. There's no way of knowing how many barrels went to the dump. I would say four or five hundred in those 12 to 15 years. Such is life in the wilderness.

Sylvia Worcester
under the dryer with her sketchpad

Marvin Allen's early barber tools
photograph by Michael Allen

# Uncle Doc's House
circa 1913

In the photograph above is my great uncle Doc Millard (my grandmother's brother) and his family. They were a prosperous farm family in Hillsboro, Texas, in the early 1900s.

## The County Seat

Jean Bartliff Brozek, an award winning journalist, told me that her father was born in the same county that I was – Palo Pinto County, Texas. Jean's grandparents were divorced, because he was a ruthless cowboy, and she was a strong-willed woman. Her grandmother earned money for her and her three boys by sewing. Jean tells about her father, Hiram, and his brother, Roy, selling fried chicken and biscuits to the travelers at the train depot. They also gathered up chunks of coal that the firemen on the train would toss out to them.

Palo Pinto, the county seat, was in the southwest part of the county, and we lived in the northwest part. It seemed like the county couldn't hold court without my father as a juror. This was a time when he either had to ride a horse or go in the buggy. It was too far away for him to come home at night. They always put the jurors up for the night in the county jail cells. Later, when we had cars, the jurors went home at night. We were really happy when he could come home, besides missing him, we were afraid. I hope my father when he was at the county seat ate some of that good fried chicken and biscuits from Hiram and Roy.

# Zelma Harrison

On March 30, 1996, my lifelong friend Zelma Harrison celebrated her 100th birthday in Altus, Oklahoma. She is definitely one of the oldest residents in our area. Zelma wasn't born in Altus. Her parents were residing near Sherman, Texas, when Zelma was born in 1886. After much persuading of family members in our area, Zelma's family decided to move here. In 1916 they put their household goods and livestock on a train bound for Altus and prepared to make to long trip to Oklahoma by covered wagon. There were no paved roads. Zelma's dad drove the wagon with a team of horses, and 20 year old Zelma followed behind in a buggy. The trip took two weeks, stopping each night and camping out in a friendly farmer's yard. They were given water and feed for the animals and water for themselves. The covered wagon was their bed and shelter. Zelma worked as a seamstress at a department store for over 40 years until the store sold out and did alterations in her home in her 90s. I've known her for 60 years. She's now 101 years old, active and looks 70 years old. I hope you enjoy Zelma's recipe.

## CORN MEAL DUMPLINS
Zelma Harrison

2½ cups corn meal
2 cups flour
2 eggs
2 Tbsp. sugar

Cook ham with bone in and save broth for corn dumplings. Pour just enough hot broth in mixture to make into patties. Drop one at a time in boiling broth and cook about 30 minutes. I put ¾ cup of meal into the broth to thicken it.

This recipe was given to me by Irene and Andrew Sadowski. I met them at a craft show in Nashville, Tennessee, where I was an exhibitor. They are from Great Britain and were on holiday here in the United States. Irene and Andrew are a delightful couple, and I had fun visiting with them.

## SCOTCH SHORTBREAD

1 lb. butter
a pinch of salt
citron peel
a few sweet almonds
1½ lb. flour
½ lb. castor sugar
caraway comfits

Mix together the flour and salt in a basin. Rub in the butter, working it in well, then add the sugar. Turn it out on a floured board and knead it into a smooth rounds. Roll out the paste into 2 small rounds about ½" thick. Pinch around the edges with the fingers. Put the shortbread on a greased baking tin and prick it all over with a fork. Cut the citron peel into fancy shapes and put two strips on the top of each cake. Sprinkle comfits over each cake and decorate with blanched split almonds. Bake in a cool oven 25-30 minutes or longer. This mixture should become very pale brown and should be firm but is still soft when hot. Do not remove from tin until slightly cool. Should the dough become soft when mixing it, let the cake stand for a while to harden before putting into oven.

# INDEX

## PORK

Baked Ham..........................................3
Baked Ham With Raisin Sauce.........4
Baked Ham With Kraut......................5
Barbequed Spare Ribs.....................8
Fried Porkchops................................6
Ham With Orange Juice and
       Catsup......................................8
History
      Aunt Lela's Fried Ham and Red-Eye
      Gravy............................................2
Pork Loin Pot Roast..........................10
Pork Roast.........................................7
Sausage Bread.................................9

## POULTRY

Stewed Chicken With Old Timey
      Rolled Dumplings...................16
Dumplings.........................................17
Buttermilk Fried Chicken..................18
Smothered Chicken...........................9
Southern Fried Chicken....................20
Chicken Gravy.................................21
Oven Chicken Salad........................22
History
      Turkey................................................12
      Chicken.............................................13
Instruction
      How To Roast The Perfect Turkey.....12
Chicken And Rice.............................23
Wild Duck..........................................23
Mrs. Mills' Roast Turkey
      And Dressing..........................14
Lou Allen's Wild Duck........................24

## BEEF

Barbequed Beef..............................29
Barbeque Sauce............................29
Barbequed Short Ribs Of Beef........30
Barb-Q Meatballs...........................31
Callene's Chili.................................33
Chicken Fried Steak........................34
Chili Con Carne............................. 33
History
The Meat Industry........................... 26
Meatballs And Tomato Gravy.........32
Meat Loaf.....................................37
Pot Roast..................................... 28
Poems......................................... 40
Rolled Roast................................. 27
Southern Hash.............................. 39
Steak Tips In Brown Gravy.............. 36
Steak San Marco... ....................... 36
Stuffed Beef Heart........................ 38
Stuffed Pepper............................. 38
Swiss Steak....................................34
The Best Ever Roast........................ 26

## FISH

Baked Fish...................................... 43
Battered Catfish.............................. 50
History
Fishing In The Past........................... 42
Instruction
Hints On Frying Fish.......................... 43
How To Boil Catfish...........................49
Mock Fish......................................44
Salmon Croquettes.........................46
Salmon Loaf.................................. 45
Seafood Casserole.........................44
Sour Cream Sole Fillet......................48
Sweet And Sour Fish........................46
Tuna Casserole.............................. 49

# FRUITS AND VEGETABLES

Aunt Lela's Corn Custard................ 56
Baked Apples.............................. 62
Baked Beans.................................. 58
Black-Eyed Peas........................... 54
Cabbage With Cheese Sauce...... 60
Cheese Apple Crisp.......................64
Fix Ahead Mashed Potatoes.......... 61
Fried Apples.................................. 63
Fried Cabbage.............................. 61
Fried Green Tomatoes.................... 55
Fried Squash With Potatoes............53
Harvard Beets............................... 59
History
      Fresh Vegetables............................66
      Fruits.........................................62
Mrs. Hickerson's Stewed Apples.....65
Onion Celeste.............................. 57
Okra Patties...................................55
Quick Baked Butter Beans.............. 58
Scalloped Apples ..........................63
Southern Fried Okra................ .......60
Wilted Lettuce.............................. 56
Yale Beets.................................... 59

# DESSERTS

Apple Brown Betty......................... 122
Aunt Lela's Vinegar Rolled
         Dumplings............................106
Barbara's Cheese Wafers.............. 113
Basic Freezer Ice Cream................135
Buttermilk Sherbet..........................138

CAKES:
Amalgamation Cake......................94
Apricot Filling For Mincemeat
         Cake.....................................79

Aunt Sue's Stacked Dried Apple
         Cake.................................... 70
Aunt Sue's Yellow Buttermilk Cake. 74
Aunt Lela's Old Timey Buttermilk
         Pound Cake........................... 72

Aunt Maude's Mincemeat Cake... 78
Camel Icing For Jam Cake............. 89
Cherry Nut Cake.................................75
Chinese Christmas Cake................. 98
Cream Cheese Pound Cake.......... 73
Chocolate Mayonnaise Cake........ 86
Chocolate Pudding Filling............... 77
Devil's Food Sour Cream Cake.......84
Eggless, Butterless, Milkless Cake.....81
Fresh Apple Cake.............................76
German Chocolate Pound Cake...76
Fruit Cocktail Cake............................91
Fudge Upside Down Cake.............84
Hoover Cake.....................................93
Japanese Fruit Cake........................92
Lane Cake.........................................96
Mississippi Mud Cake........................90
Mock Angel Food Cake................. 87
My Mother's Cake............................99
My Old Standby Loaf Or
        Layer Cake............................. 86
Pineapple Upside Down Cake....... 80
Prune Cake........................................ 97
Punch Bowl Cake............................. 88
Tennessee Jam Cake........................88
Texas Pecan Cake........................... 83
Upside Down Chocolate Cake...... 82

Deluxe Bread Pudding...................133
Easy Apple Dumplings................... 103
Fruit Cobbler.....................................120
History
        Aunt Sue..............................................68
        Cobbler and Canning...................119
        The Gettysburg Address............... 129
Instruction
        Helpful Hints For Making Freezer Ice
        Cream............................................. 134
Minnie White's Bake Custard........109
Peach Sherbet............................... 138
Persimmon Pudding...................... 131

PIES:

Aunt Maude's Rhubarb Pie.......... 111
Aunt Sue's Sour Cream Apple Pie.115
Banana Pie................................ 127
Basic Cream Pie....................... 121
Blueberry Pie............................. 100
Buttermilk Pie............................ 110
Chocolate Bourbon Pecan Pie..... 126
Chocolate Cream Pie.................. 122
Date Pie.................................... 127
Glazed Apple Pie....................... 116
Fried Pies..................................103
Jeff Davis Pie............................. 128
Lemon Chess Pie....................... 102
Marie Mills' Two Crust
          Pineapple Pie...................115
Marie Mills' Perfect Meringue....... 112
Mincemeat Pie........................... 100
Mrs. Mills' Pumpkin Custard Pie......114
Oatmeal Pie............................... 110
Old Timey Chess Pie.................... 102
Pearl Sloan's Big Custard Pie.........107
Pecan Pie.................................. 110
Pie Crust For Two Crust 9" Pie.........117
Prize Winning Peachy Pie...............104
Shoofly Pie................................ 124
Sugar Pie.................................. 123
Two Crust Cherry Pie.....................125
Weepless Meringue.......................113

Refrigerator Vanilla Ice Cream......136
Rich Biscuit Dough....................... 120
Strawberry Banana Ice Cream..... 101
Sweetened Condensed Milk ........101
Sweet Potato Pudding.................. 132
Suet Pudding............................. 130
Vanilla Ice Milk............................ 137
Vinegar Rolls.............................. 108

## COOKIES AND CANDIES

Aunt Bill's Brown Candy..................156
Aunt Lela's Sour Cream Cookies......144
Aunt Lela's Tea Cakes....................140

Aunt Mae's Tea Cakes..................... 143
Aunt Sue's Date Loaf Candy......... 154
Aunt Sue's Southern Pralines.........148
Best Peanut Butter Fudge.............. 155
Candied Orange Peel................... 152
Christmas Candy........................... 155
Easy Date Cookies........................145
Kisses............................................. 141
Marie Mills' Creamy Candy...........151
Marie Mills' Oatmeal Cookies........142
Mary Alice's Peanut Patties.......... 160
Nova Crow's Pecan Pralines.........159
Oatmeal Cookies........................... 147
Old Timey Fudge...........................153
Peanut Brittle................................150
Peanut Butter Cookies...................141
Pineapple Cookies........................146
Saucepan Pralines........................ 158
Sugar Cookies...............................146
Tea Cakes.....................................148

## BREADS

All Bran Muffins..............................186
All Bran Rolls..................................188
Apricot Upside Down Muffins........188
Aunt Sue's Baking Powder
       Biscuits...................................173
Aunt Sue's Blueberry Muffins..........187
Aunt Sue's Everlasting Yeast
       Starter...................................164
Banana Nut Bread..........................182
Basic Pancake Batter.....................178
Buttermilk Biscuits...........................176
Buttermilk Pancakes.......................179
Carrot Bread................................. 184
Corn Bread.................................... 181
Corn Bread Kentucky Style............182
Easy Rolls......................................174
Everlasting Rolls.............................171
Egg Butter..................................... 185
Egg Cake...................................... 189

History

    The Staff Of Life.............................. 162

    Waffles............................................... 180

Hominy Grit Spoon Bread.............190

Hush Puppies.....................................177

Icebox Yeast Bread........................ 168

Instruction

    How To Knead Yeast Bread...........165

    How To Keep And Use Starter.......166

    Rules For Making Yeast Dough......167

    How To Toast Bread.........................176

Just Plain Yeast Bread..................... 170

Kush.....................................................177

Light Bread........................................ 165

My Favorite Pancake Syrup...........179

Nut Bread........................................... 183

Pecan Waffles.................................. 181

Potato Split Biscuits..........................175

Sour Dough Biscuits..........................172

Sweet Milk Rolls..................................172

Sweet Potato Biscuit....................... 175

Sour Dough Starter...........................169

Zucchini Bread................................. 184

## SALADS AND SOUPS

Aunt Lela's Prepared Mustard......195

Aunt Sue's Winter Waldorf Salad..196

Cabbage Christmas Salad............197

Chicken Salad................................. 195

History................................................192

Instruction

    Tips On Tossed Green Salad

    With French Dressing............. 194

Old Time Potato Salad....................193

Tuna Salad........................................ 196

Olive And Egg Salad.......................198

Avocado Salad................................198

Cream Fruit Salad ...........................199

Frozen Surprise Salad...................... 200

Strawberry And Cream...................200

Corn Chowder..................................201

Three Week Slaw.............................. 202

Cabbage Patch Stew.....................203

243

Marie Mills' Chicken Soup..............203
Marvin Allen's Stew........................204

## RELISHES AND PRESERVES

Aunt Lela's Peach Preserves.........218
Aunt Sue's Cantaloupe Pickles.....206
Beet Pickles.....................................210
Crystal Pickles.................................210
Cucumber Cinnamon Rings.........215
Dill Pickles...................................... 209
Fourteen Day Pickles...........................207
Kosher Dills.....................................208
Instruction
      How To Preserve A Husband.........214
Molly's Squash Pickles....................213
Orange Marmalade.......................218
Orange Sweet Pickles....................214
Peach Sweet Pickles......................210
Pickled Walnuts..............................211
Plain Sour Pickles............................209
Poem
      What Can I Give?...........................220
Pumpkin Preserves......................... 216
Strawberry Preserves......................217
Strawberry Sun Preserves.............. 219
Squash Pickles................................212
Sweet Pickles.................................. 209

## MEMORIES

So Much To Do............................... 222
Snow Ice Cream.............................224
My Brother Charlie..........................226
Entertainment.................................228
The Horse And The Sweater.......... 229
One Christmas................................ 229
We Saved Everything!....................230
Our Early Household......................231
The Beauty Shop............................ 231
Uncle Doc's House.........................234
The County Seat.............................234
Zelma Harrison................................235
Corn Meal Dumplings....................235
Scotch Shortbread........................236

# THELMA ALLEN
## PERSONAL APPEARANCES

When her schedule permits, Thelma Allen would like to talk to your group about the writing of her cookbooks, her memories and how-to-start a new business in your retirement years.

Thelma is available for special appearances for your:
> Church group
> Social club
> Civic organization
> In-store promotion
> Radio and television talk show
> Business

# SWEET YESTERDAY
## FUND RAISING PROGRAM

The "Recipes From Sweet Yesterday" cookbooks are excellent products that can be sold by your group for your fund raising needs.

## FOR APPEARANCE AVAILABILITY AND INFORMATION ON OUR FUND RAISING PROGRAM, CONTACT:

Michael Allen
Michael Allen Entertainment
P. O. Box 111510
Nashville, TN 37222
email: michael@sweetyesterday.com

Visit our Web site:
**www.sweetyesterday.com**

# OTHER SWEET YESTERDAY COOKBOOKS

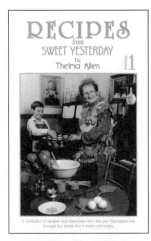

Recipes From Sweet Yesterday
        Volume One
238 recipes
196 pages
Binding: soft cover, plastic comb-bound
ISBN: 0-9668322-0-5

Recipes From Sweet Yesterday
        Volume Two
245 recipes
232 pages
Binding: soft cover, plastic comb-bound
ISBN: 0-9668322-1-3

Recipes From Sweet Yesterday
        Volume Four
236 recipes
245 pages
Binding: soft cover, plastic comb-bound
ISBN: 0-9668322-4-8

These titles can be ordered
from Sweet Yesterday,
online at sweetyesterday.com,
online at barnesandnoble.com,
and at any bookstore.

You will enjoy hearing

# Thelma Allen
## tell
her memories in these
## "Stories From Sweet Yesterday"
CDs and audio cassette.

Thelma tells her memories from the pre-Depression era through the World War II years and today on her audio CDs and cassette. When she paints word pictures, your imagination will put you back in time.

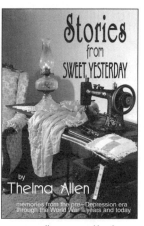

CD package includes two CDs—
Volume One and Volume Two

one audio cassette tape

## Stories on CDs and cassette includes:

Family Background
Recipes
Days On The Farm
Just For Fun
Crops
Clothes
School
Christmas
Our First Car
Outhouse
Don't Throw Anything Away

Homemade Ice Cream
Conditions At Home
Dinner On The Ground
Going To Church
Moving To Oklahoma
The Tornado Of 1928
The Depression Days
World War II
Chores
Songs
Closing Thoughts

88 minutes

See order form in this book.

# Visit our Web site at

## www.sweetyesterday.com

- **Free Recipes**

- **Recipe Sharing** (with our Web site visitors)

- **Latest News** From Sweet Yesterday

- Thelma Allen **Personal Appearances**

- Product **News** & Latest **Updates**
  - "Recipes From Sweet Yesterday" cookbooks
  - "Stories From Sweet Yesterday" audio products
  - New Products

# *Thanks*

for purchasing the

## Recipes From Sweet Yesterday

cookbooks.

We know you will enjoy your books.
**You may want to purchase some more copies
for *gifts for friends and relatives!***
Here's a *checklist* for you to use.
Write volume number by name.

## Order Products (order form on the next pages or online with your credit cards)

☐ Birthday gifts for:                                      Date needed:

      (name)_____  _____

      (name)_____  _____

      (name)_____  _____

☐ Wedding gifts for:

      (name)_____  _____

      (name)_____  _____

      (name)_____  _____

☐ Christmas gifts for:

      (name)_____  _____

      (name)_____  _____

      (name)_____  _____

☐ Graduation gifts for:

      (name)_____  _____

      (name)_____  _____

      (name)_____  _____

☐ Mother's Day gifts for:

      (name)_____  _____

      (name)_____  _____

      (name)_____  _____

# OTHER SWEET YESTERDAY COOKBOOKS

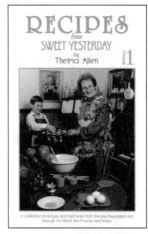

Recipes From Sweet Yesterday
  Volume One
238 recipes
196 pages
Binding: soft cover, plastic comb-bound
ISBN: 0-9668322-0-5

Recipes From Sweet Yesterday
  Volume Two
245 recipes
232 pages
Binding: soft cover, plastic comb-bound
ISBN: 0-9668322-1-3

Recipes From Sweet Yesterday
  Volume Four
236 recipes
245 pages
Binding: soft cover, plastic comb-bound
ISBN: 0-9668322-4-8

These titles can be ordered
from Sweet Yesterday,
online at sweetyesterday.com,
online at barnesandnoble.com,
and at any bookstore.

# ORDER EXTRA COPIES
of the
## "SWEET YESTERDAY" COOKBOOKS
and the
## "STORIES FROM SWEET YESTERDAY"
### CDs and CASSETTE

NO. OF COPIES___**VOLUME 1** @ $10.$^{00}$ each
NO. OF COPIES___**VOLUME 2** @ $10.$^{00}$ each
NO. OF COPIES___**VOLUME 3** @ $10.$^{00}$ each
NO. OF COPIES___**VOLUME 4** @ $10.$^{00}$ each
NO. OF COPIES___**STORIES CDs** @ $10.$^{00}$ (for 2 CDs, Vol. & Vol. 2)
NO. OF COPIES___**STORIES CASSETTE** @ $7.$^{00}$ each

SUBTOTAL_____

Add 9.25% sales tax (Tenn. residents only)_____
Postage and handling for 1st product - $4$^{25}$_____
    P & H for each additional product - $1$^{25}$_____

**TOTAL**_____

ORDERED BY_____

STREET/APT. NO._____

CITY/STATE/ZIP_____

PHONE (___)_____

**MAKE YOUR CHECK OR MONEY ORDER TO: SWEET YESTERDAY.**

**PLEASE MAIL THIS ORDER FORM WITH YOUR PAYMENT TO:**

Sweet Yesterday
P.O. Box 111510
Nashville, TN 37222

Please allow 2 weeks for delivery and always on time
for special occasions. All prices are subject to change
without notice.

# OTHER SWEET YESTERDAY COOKBOOKS

Recipes From Sweet Yesterday
          Volume One
238 recipes
196 pages
Binding: soft cover, plastic comb-bound
ISBN: 0-9668322-0-5

Recipes From Sweet Yesterday
          Volume Two
245 recipes
232 pages
Binding: soft cover, plastic comb-bound
ISBN: 0-9668322-1-3

Recipes From Sweet Yesterday
          Volume Four
236 recipes
245 pages
Binding: soft cover, plastic comb-bound
ISBN: 0-9668322-4-8

These titles can be ordered
from Sweet Yesterday,
online at sweetyesterday.com,
online at barnesandnoble.com,
and at any bookstore.

# ORDER EXTRA COPIES
of the
## "SWEET YESTERDAY" COOKBOOKS
and the
## "STORIES FROM SWEET YESTERDAY"
## CDs and CASSETTE

NO. OF COPIES___**VOLUME 1** @ $10.$^{00}$ each
NO. OF COPIES___**VOLUME 2** @ $10.$^{00}$ each
NO. OF COPIES___**VOLUME 3** @ $10.$^{00}$ each
NO. OF COPIES___**VOLUME 4** @ $10.$^{00}$ each
NO. OF COPIES___**STORIES CDs** @ $10.$^{00}$ (for 2 CDs, Vol. & Vol. 2)
NO. OF COPIES___**STORIES CASSETTE** @ $7.$^{00}$ each

SUBTOTAL_____

Add 9.25% sales tax (Tenn. residents only)_____
Postage and handling for 1st product - $4$^{25}$_____
 P & H for each additional product - $1$^{25}$_____

**TOTAL**_____

ORDERED BY_____

STREET/APT. NO._____

CITY/STATE/ZIP_____

PHONE (____)_____

**MAKE YOUR CHECK OR MONEY ORDER TO: SWEET YESTERDAY.**

**PLEASE MAIL THIS ORDER FORM WITH YOUR PAYMENT TO:**

Sweet Yesterday
P.O. Box 111510
Nashville, TN 37222

Please allow 2 weeks for delivery and always on time
for special occasions. All prices are subject to change
without notice.